BLOODY BRI[

HISTORY

DERBY

BLOODY BRITISH HISTORY

HISTORY

DERBY

PAUL SULLIVAN

For Jay Sullivan, Derbyshire's finest

———∽∞∽———

The man that killed this ram, Sir, was up to his eyes in blood,
And four and twenty butcher boys were washed away in the flood.
('The Derby Ram', traditional folk song)

The History Press
The Mill, Brimscombe Port
Stroud, Gloucestershire, GL5 2QG
www.thehistorypress.co.uk

British Library Cataloguing in Publication Data.
A catalogue record for this book is available from the British Library.

ISBN 978 0 7524 6309 4

Typesetting and origination by The History Press
Printed in Great Britain

CONTENTS

ACKNOWLEDGEMENTS

Humble thanks to the following, who enabled this book to be written:

Marlene and Terry Sullivan (aka Mam and Dad), who looked after everyone while I got on with it.

Magda Bezdekova and our children Jan and Theo, who ignored me while I wrestled with the Muse.

Cate Ludlow at The History Press, who came up with the idea and gave me the go-ahead.

Jay Sullivan, who lives in Derbyshire and makes sure that a large part of me does too.

Andy Savage, of *www.derbyphotos.co.uk*, who kindly donated the modern photographs in this book.

THE LEGION THAT LOST ITS HEAD

ARRIVING IN THE region during the first century AD, the Romans founded a new settlement and named it 'Derventio'. It was built at a strategic location, near a major river on the north-south artery of Britain. Doubtless the invaders expected staunch resistance from the blood-curdling Britons that got here before them, but archaeology suggests that not a great deal happened (apart from a rebuilding of the fort once every century). It was a bit like one of those episodes of *Time Team* where nothing turns up in Trench 3. For a while, at least...

Prior to the Roman invasion, the southern chunk of modern Derbyshire, along with the broad region encompassing Nottinghamshire, Leicestershire and Lincolnshire, was ruled by a British tribe called the Corieltauvi (aka the Coritani). These particular Britons were not noted for their skills on the battlefield. Their chief mark on posterity is their generally rather dull coins: minimal decoration, and plain letters naming their various monarchs.

At the time of the Roman takeover, the ruler of the Corieltauvi was Volisios, who ruled the region from Corieltauvorum (Leicester). He appears to have offered no resistance, and this region may have been the Romans' easiest conquest in Britain.

A war-like Briton, spear at the ready.

7

Julius Caesar invading Britain. He described a nation of warriors stained blue with woad, which gave them 'a more horrible aspect in battle'. Hobbies of the Britons allegedly included filling a reed man with living people and setting it on fire.

It is likely that Volisios actually welcomed the newcomers, viewing them as an armed-to-the-teeth guard against the actively martial tribes surrounding him, including the Brigantes to the north and the Catuvellauni to the south. It was a largely agricultural lifestyle here in the Midlands, and the Corieltauvi probably fended off attack down the years by providing food for their neighbours at bargain rates – the cut-price supermarket of their day.

ROMANS SHOWN THE RED CARD

The site the Romans had chosen was not a settlement beforehand – there were just a few farmers to complain about what the new neighbours were building in their backyard. On one side of the river, the Romans founded Derventio, building a fort on the opposite bank – which was stuffed with soldiers and hardware, as befitted an important crossing point on the Derwent (after which Derventio was named, probably meaning 'place of white oaks').

This fort was intended to guard no less than five Roman roads, including the important south-west to north-east highway Ryknild Street (surviving, in name at least, at Rykneld Road in the modern city of Derby). But the generals soon realised that there was not actually much of a threat to repel.

A pottery and ironworks were established in Derventio, making kitchenware and swords (but presumably having

DERBY FOOTBALL: ORIGIN OF THE HEADER

The Shrovetide street football that formerly rampaged through the streets of Derby (and which still survives 12 miles north-west at Ashbourne) began as a commemoration of the British victory against the Romans of Derventio in AD 275, and the slicing off and kicking around of Roman heads afterwards.

The authorities tried many times to suppress the sport of football. In 1747, an outbreak of foot and mouth disease was used as the excuse, a proclamation from the Mayor ordering: 'that no riotous or tumultuous meeting of any persons (and especially of foreigners at this unhappy time of contagion amongst horned cattle) do appear for the purpose [of football].'

But the game still had almost 100 years to go before suppression. According to a description in White's *Directory of Derbyshire*: 'About noon the ball was tossed up; this was seized by the strongest and most active men, the rest closed in upon them, and a solid mass was formed, the struggle was then violent, and the motion of this immense human mass heaving to and fro, was tremendous and appalling... The numbers engaged exceeded 1,000, and the streets were crowded with spectators, the shops were closed and boarded and business suspended.' Another historian added, 'Broken shins, broken heads, torn coats, and lost hats are among the minor accidents of this fearful contest, and it frequently happens that persons fall in consequence of the intensity of the pressure, fainting and bleeding beneath the feet of the surrounding mob... A Frenchman passing through Derby remarked, that if Englishmen called this playing, it would be impossible to say what they would call fighting.'

The whistle was blown for the last time in Derby in 1839 when the game descended into mayhem, the Riot Act was read out, and the army sent everyone off.

little cause to use the latter *in situ*), and presaging Derby's later role as a major industrial centre. But by the mid-third century, the soldiers seem to have had a minimal presence in the sleepy, peaceful little town.

Bad move! Local legend records that in AD 275, the Britons – possibly the Brigantes or Catuvellauni rather than the meek locals – finally turned violent and stormed Derventio, killing all the Romans they could find. After their victory, they chopped off their enemies' heads (a favourite pastime of the Celtic tribes) and used them as balls, inventing the game of football in the process. They didn't stay to consolidate their conquest after the full-time whistle, though, and Derventio stood empty after the crowds had gone home.

Suitably miffed, the Romans stormed back in, but found no one to hack to pieces. They rebuilt the town with an encircling stone wall, just in case. At last it looked as if those locally made swords were going to come in handy... but nothing happened. By the end of the fourth century, the Romans had left Derventio to the farmers and their goats. It was later known as Little Chester – the modern Chester Green area of Derby.

800

ALKMUND: SAINT AND HERO. ALLEGEDLY

IN TIMES OF anarchy and civil war, recorded history tends to go into meltdown, and in the aftermath a collection of names and events emerges – not necessarily complete, probably not in the right order, and not at all reliable in any way. Such is the background to the tale of Alkmund, Patron Saint of Derby, Prince of Northumbria and Bane of the Danes. His story probably didn't go something a little like this...

In the mid-eighth century, the reign of the northern Anglo-Saxon Kings was facing premature closure following a succession of invasions from Danish Vikings. Wave after wave of sword-wielding marauders stormed the beaches between the Thames and the Tweed, and in Northumbria things were truly 'grim up north'. King Alcred, who reigned in that vast kingdom between AD 765 and 774, placed his younger son Alkmund out of harm's way in the care of Pictish allies, in the north of what is now Scotland. He spent most of his reign attacking and fending off large sections of the Danish army in the company of his eldest son, Osred.

The Danes, however, proved to be the least of young Alkmund's troubles. He became the legitimate heir to the Northumbrian Crown in 790, following the murder of his brother, Osred, by Ethelred.

Ethelred was head of one of the three rival royal dynasties in the kingdom, and had seized the Crown in 774. But when Ethelred was murdered in 796, Alkmund was passed over in favour of yet another prince, Eardwulf, who had been given the thumbs-up by the Archbishop of York in June that year (in spite of forsaking his wife and installing a mistress in her place). Eardwulf became King in Alkmund's place.

BACK FROM THE DEAD

Having bloodied his sword against the Vikings in many battles alongside his Northumbrian, Mercian and Pictish allies, Alkmund now had a dead brother to avenge and a usurped throne to win back.

However, removing Eardwulf from power proved to be rather difficult. According to one legend, Eardwulf had once been executed – but he returned from the grave while no one was looking. This was declared a divinely engineered miracle, and it caused King Ethelred (before he was murdered) to exile Eardwulf from the kingdom. But after the King's death, Eardwulf was not only back but installed on the throne.

Romantic, patriotic, religious biographers have claimed that Alkmund eventually claimed back his throne, and scored many victories against the Danes before he was treacherously murdered by them in AD 819. His fame and popularity meant he was eventually declared a martyr, and he was given the fast track to saintdom. Victorian hagiographers called him meek, humble, affable, and generous to a fault when it came to succouring the poor – standard attributes for any saint whose actual history is shrouded in Dark Age uncertainty.

A very downbeat, parallel strand of history says that the hero-prince-saint was assassinated by Eardwulf in the year 800, along with other Northumbrian noblemen who might be in a position one day to usurp the King. Other versions say that Alkmund *did* actually reign at some stage. Then again, there are three other Kings listed as rulers of Northumbria in this period too, so the case remains unsolved.

SAINT COMES MARCHING IN

Whatever the truth, Alkmund's body was eventually laid to rest in Derby, and a shrine was built around his bones, with St Alkmund's church plonked on top. Miracles followed, both here and at nearby St Alkmund's Well (still flowing on River Street), which magically appeared when the coffin-carrying procession paused to rest: healing waters allegedly sprang forth, and pilgrims thereafter beat a path to the town, much to the benefit of the ecclesiastical coffers.

The kingdom of Mercia opposed the rule of Eardwulf in neighbouring Northumbria. But the King fended off many rebellions, and even when he was deposed he managed to win the support of the Pope and one of the most powerful rulers of the whole millennium, Charles the Great of Bohemia, aka Charlemagne. With these backers he was soon reinstated

Female Pict: Alkmund stayed with this fearsome race as a boy.

on the throne, where he remained until his death in 810. Meanwhile, the tides of northern English civil war continued to ebb and flow.

This was insane, in retrospect, as the infighting meant that Mercians and Northumbrians were taking their eye off the real enemies, the Danes and the Wessex men. Within a few years, both kingdoms would be held not by the heirs of Alkmund and Eardwulf, but by a combination of raping and pillaging – well, reaping and ploughing, actually – Vikings, and the West Saxons, whose King, Edmund, won Derby back from the Danes in 944.

ST ALKMUND'S CHURCH: BYPASSING DERBY'S PATRON SAINT

Alkmund is Derby's patron saint, an elevated position which was marked in peculiar fashion in 1968 by the demolition of his church and its surrounding Georgian square (the city's only such feature) between Bridgegate and Queen Street.

Developers argued that the church was a Victorian edifice of no great architectural value; and, besides, a commemorative plaque was to be placed near the site on the ungodly inner ring-road that rose in its place, so how could anybody possibly complain?

It was an ignominious end for the succession of eponymous edifices that had stood on that spot for the last 1,100 years – but there was a small consolation lying there in the excavator's rubble.

A tenth-century Saxon coffin, immediately said to be the centrepiece of the saint-king's long-lost shrine, was disinterred, and can be seen today in the city museum. Modern historians favour the theory that it is actually the tomb of Ealdorman Ethelwulf, killed in 871 during the Viking wars and buried in Derby.

The demolition of St Alkmund's church inspired anger that hasn't entirely died down yet; and the construction in the 1970s of a modern 'St Alkmund's' on Kedleston Road did little to placate those who saw the whole affair as short-sighted town developers' vandalism.

St Mary's Bridge; St Alkmund's church was once at the end.

ETHELFLEDA: MERCIA'S KILLER QUEEN

POPULAR ENGLISH HISTORY has done a great disservice to this island's pre-Victorian female leaders. Queens Matilda and Jane Grey get written out of official monarch lists, and the likes of Mary I, Mary II, Anne, and even Elizabeth I, are portrayed as fascinating but essentially irrelevant aberrations on the journey from one King to another.

But the greatest historical crime of all is the hushing-up of tenth-century sword-swinging Queen Ethelfleda, 'Lady of Mercia' and conqueror of Danish Derby. Ethelfleda is like something from the script of a historical soap opera. Her feats rank with those of Boadicea, and she died as the undefeated, undisputed Queen of northern England. It's time to set her back where she belongs, on the blood-spattered pedestal labelled 'Best English Queen Ever!'

Ethelfleda was the daughter of King Alfred the Great, born in 872 at the height of the Danes' power in an England all but submerged by the Viking onslaught. They ruled everything north of London, and had a stranglehold on the south too. Derby was one of their chief towns in the conquered kingdom of Mercia. By AD 876, the rump of the English resistance in Wessex – and with it, the whole concept of England and English – was holed up

Gravely misrepresented: the grave of Elizabeth I, one of the few female regents to be remembered by history.

in the Somerset marshes, burning apocryphal cakes and wondering how on earth it could muster enough of an army to crawl back out of the swamp.

Around the time of Ethelfleda's sixth birthday, Alfred somehow managed to

Above *Alfred – the Grate! King Alfred letting the cakes burn.*

Left *King Alfred the Great.*

raise a large enough force to confront and defeat the Vikings under their King Guthrum who, horrified by the violence of the slaughter and rivers of blood that washed the battlefield, agreed to let Alfred rule Wessex without Danish interference.

But the Danes still ruled most of the roost, and their stronghold at Derby was actually boosted by Alfred himself when he chose to repatriate the defeated Wessex Vikings in the town. This was just storing up problems for Ethelfleda in the future.

DERBY: FRONTIER AND WARZONE

In 886, Saxon Mercia was revived when Alfred conquered Danish London and returned it to the Mercian King, Ethelred. To seal the deal Ethelred married Ethelfleda,

MERCIA UPON US!

— ∞∞ —

*   Mercia – meaning 'border people' – was one of the original Saxon territories stitched together from the corpses of several British kingdoms following their defeat by Anglo-Saxon invaders from the north-west coast of Europe (south of Scandinavia, chiefly the north of modern Germany).
*   Mercia was a huge kingdom, stretching from the Humber to the Thames and bordered by the East Angles to the east, various Saxon kingdoms to the south, Northumberland to the north, and the surviving Britons to the west, in what the cheeky invaders labelled 'Wales', meaning 'the foreigners'.
*   It was elbowed from much of its former territory by the Viking-held 'Danelaw' region during the ninth and tenth centuries.
*   Its most powerful rulers were King Offa (AD 626–55), King Penda (AD 757–96) and Ethelfleda, 'Lady of the Mercians' (AD 902–18).
*   Tamworth was the Mercian capital, and Derby was one of the other principal towns.
*   After its Danish occupants had been routed by Ethelfleda, Mercia was conquered, ironically, by Wessex Kings as part of the consolidation of the English nation. The last fully independent Mercian monarch was Edgar, who reigned from AD 955–9 before his kingdom was subsumed again by Wessex.

— ∞∞ —

then at the grand old age of fourteen. She soon won fame for her fighting skills and extraordinary intelligence. As a reflection of this, King Alfred's son and successor, Edward ('the Elder'), sent his own son and heir Athelstan to Ethelfleda for education – notably training in the arts of military prowess and diplomacy.

By her late teens, Ethelfleda was renowned as a fearless warrior. People said she had undergone such pains and near-death experiences in childbirth that life held no more terrors for her. They also whispered that she had turned her back on the marital bed, favouring martial bedlam instead – 'better adapted to reduce than augment the race', as eighteenth-century historian William Hutton put it.

Viking Derby was impressed with none of this. Bolstered by reinforcements from the Danish homeland in 892, the natives reached once again for their swords and shields. War brought a procession of short-lived captains to the city, Danish and Saxon alike, who ruled with all the uncertainty of a sheriff in one of the dodgier frontier towns of the Wild West.

According to Hutton: 'The Danes chiefly inhabited the North of England; and the Saxons the south. They approached each other through Derby, as the medium, which often felt the horrors of robbery and butchery.'

In 902, a debilitating illness overtook Ethelfleda's husband King Ethelred. She was now undisputed ruler, Queen of Mercia, with the blessing of her staunch ally and brother Edward the Elder, who ruled the south following Alfred's demise in 899.

DERBY DISAPPEARS

Ethelfleda's record as Mercian ruler is amazing: she repulsed Norse invaders at Chester; mounted a joint invasion of 100 per cent Danish East Anglia with brother Edward, bringing back the relics of St Oswald; and crushed the last wave of fresh Danish invaders at Tettenhall in Lincolnshire.

St Oswald was the most famous and revered English saint at this point in history. He was the son of Ethelfrid the

Ravager and the grandson of 'the Burner', and reigned as King of the Northumbrians from AD 634 to 642. He died on the battlefield at the age of thirty-eight, and vengeful Mercian King Penda cut off his hands and head and stuck them on poles. They remained there for a whole year, until they were rescued by relic-spotters. The head went into St Oswald's coffin, now at Durham Cathedral, and the hands to Bamburgh. The bits of dirt that Oswald had bled into were carefully gathered up, and the stake which had carried his head was cut up into pocket-sized pieces. Both types of relic allegedly had healing properties. One of the saint's hands had been saved from the usual ravages of death by divine blessing, and never rotted away: it was kept in Northumbria so it could be kissed by pilgrims. It was later stolen by the monks of Peterborough Cathedral. Eventually, the rest of Oswald's body was dug up: the bones were put in a casket covered with gold, silver and jewels, and it was this that was eventually rescued by the Mercian Queen.

To show the Anglo-Danes that she bore no malice in spite of all the bloodshed, Ethelfleda met their Derby contingent and persuaded them, and the rest of the Danelaw, to unite with her against Norwegian invaders. These Norsemen had settlements in the west of England and Wales, sweeping in from their Irish bases as well as from the north. The united Mercians and Danes signed war pacts with the Scots and Welsh, and the Norwegians were battered back to their longboats.

Such friendships are all well and good in the face of imminent war. But, when peace was restored, Ethelfleda decided that Mercia needed better fortification. It also needed a certain town called Derby, which for too long had been a melting pot of Viking skulduggery.

In 917, having fortified all the Saxon bits of Mercia, Ethelfleda headed for the badlands of Derby, where the bloodiest battle in the city's history took place. With an army answering to no one but her, she marched over the Derwent at what is now St Mary's Bridge, and caught the Danes by surprise, routing their hasty defence and forcing the battle into the area enclosed by the town walls. The fighting was concentrated west of the modern Osmaston

Coin of Edward the Elder, who conquered Colchester whilst Ethelfleda was seizing Derby.

DANELAW: VIKINGS UNITED

The after-match reports wax lyrical about King Alfred the Great's performance against the Danes in AD 886. But the bloody match he played that year against opposing captain Guthrum was full of English own goals.

A vast chunk of the country, from the Thames to Scotland, was retained by the various Scandinavian players. The largest chunk by far was 'the Danelaw' (where, as the name suggests, Danish law prevailed). It included the vast former kingdom of Northumbria, stretching from the Humber to the Scottish borders; East Anglia; the south-east Midlands, including London; and a Midlands stronghold centred on five powerful boroughs: Derby, Nottingham, Leicester, Lincoln and Stamford.

Final score: Vikings 8, English 1.

Road, and the streets were soon ploughed to red mud, strewn with blood and bodies. Ethelfleda lost four of her best thanes and hundreds of foot soldiers, but the Danes lost many more, and the mainly wooden city was reduced to ash and rubble, only the castle offering the routed men brief protection. But this was soon taken by the Queen, and most of its defenders were slaughtered. As far as this battle was concerned, the fewer Viking survivors, the better.

VIKINGS UNDER THE BED

When eventually its shattered walls and buildings rose again, Derby was Saxon once more – or English, as the children of King Alfred now liked to call themselves and their possessions.

While Ethelfleda was flattening Derby, King Edward the Elder had conquered Danish Colchester, another key Danelaw town. In the following year, the Queen made known her intentions to march on Leicester to consolidate Mercia further; but the Vikings saw her coming and surrendered without bloodshed. The majority of the Midland-dwelling Danes now bowed to Ethelfleda as their overlord; and things were escalating further, even Viking HQ York capitulating, when death snatched the mighty Queen away.

Ethelfleda's name was invoked in hushed awe for several generations in Derby; but in other parts of the country she was soon forgotten. And even in Derby itself, memory of the town's era as a dangerous Danish frontier town outlasted memory of the Queen. As Hutton noted in 1791:

The dread of their cruelties continued upon the mind for ages; nay, it was not totally worn off even so late as my infancy; the elder child, already frightened, informed the younger, 'that the Danes would arrive, enter every house, and murder all the people...'

1066

DANE AND OUT

IN 1048 THERE was an earthquake in Derby, followed by drought and famine which killed man and beast alike. Much of the tinder-dry land around the town was destroyed by uncontrollable wild fires, as if an irate god had dropped an anachronistic cigarette end, taking a further toll on life and livelihood. When it was all over, the Anglo-Danish inhabitants of Derbyshire could have been forgiven for thinking that the century's worst deprivations were in the past.

No such luck. Slaughter, conquest and decimation lay ahead, starting with the death of English King Edward the Confessor in 1066. His two would-be successors, Harold Godwinson and William the Bastard, had different ideas about how the future of the island should pan out. And one way or another, Derby was going to bear all the ravages of the forthcoming wars.

The town, with its 200-year-old Danish roots, was instantly loyal to Harold who, as his name suggests, was from one of the Viking dynasties. When this ill-fated King set off north to defend the kingdom against yet another Viking army, this time led by Norwegian Harald Hardrada and Harold's own brother Tostig (plus mixed Norse and Danish allies), most able-bodied Derbeians followed him. After victory at Stamford Bridge, it was small consolation to Derby's men that their home was en route to the next battle down in Sussex, where William was due to land with his Normandy army. The Derby men barely had time to say goodbye to their families before being dragged south.

Hundreds of years later, in 1807, a hoard of 270 silver coins and other pieces of silver was found buried near the site of the Stamford Bridge battle: this was thought to be plunder from the corpses left that day, perhaps buried by one of Derby's soldiers as he marched south to Hastings – never to return. According to some sources, there was more gold left on the field than twelve men could carry. The battle was also marked by a famous stand over the bridge, where one man held off Harold's entire army for more than three hours. He killed more than forty men before he was brought down by an arrow. Five or six hundred boats brought over the attacking army; twenty boats were all that was needed to carry Hardrada's army home.

WILLIAM AND HARRY

When Harold's army marched towards Hastings, it took most of Derby with it:

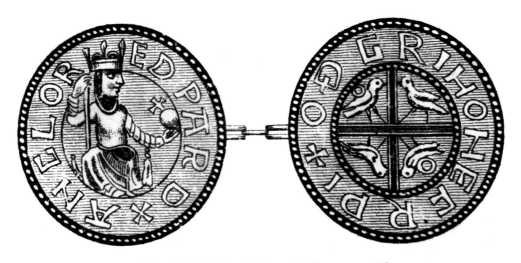

Coin of Edward 'the Confessor', whose death began a new civil war.

Coin of Harold I: hundreds of coins from this era were secretly buried near Stamford Bridge.

HARRYING OF THE NORTH

William sent an army north with the sole purpose of destroying everyone and everything. Villages were burnt, livestock was killed, foodstocks were destroyed, the land was razed and poisoned with salt, and every means of continued survival was removed. More than 100,000 people died as a direct or indirect result of this 'Harrying of the North', and others were reduced to cannibalism.

Even pro-Norman chroniclers were horrified, eleventh-century Orderic Vitalis declaring, 'I have often praised William in this book, but I can say nothing good about this brutal slaughter. God will punish him.' The 1086 Domesday Book resorts frequently to the poignant phrase *vaste est*, 'it has been laid waste', in its assessment of the harried regions. Large swathes of Derbyshire are described in his way.

William I, whose army razed Derbyshire.

the town is said to have emptied itself of all men capable of wielding a weapon. Off they went to that fateful field north of Hastings; and not many lived to see it renamed Battle. But the victorious William did not let it end there. Of Viking stock himself (the dukedom of Normandy and its resident Normans being named after the 'North men' who conquered it), he may well have seen this as the last phase of a couple of centuries of Viking civil wars. Harold was down and out, and former Danish strongholds, such as Derby and York, would have to be razed to prevent the rebellions from reaching critical mass.

This was the philosophy behind William's 'Harrying of the North' policy, 1069–71, during which the famous Norman Yoke was applied in the most bloody and ruthless manner imaginable. While William's rivals cowered, and while his own master the King of France nodded approvingly, the Conqueror proved what a Bastard he really was. The brunt of the attack fell on the land north of the Humber, but Derby was flattened too, and the population of the county had halved by the time the Domesday Book was compiled in 1086, with many formerly thriving areas described as 'wasteland'.

And that was the end of Anglo-Danish Derby. A fully English identity lay ahead, with a succession of Norman-descended aristocrats ruling the region, carrying the title Earl of Derby from the twelfth century onwards.

THE EARL-Y YEARS OF DERBY

WHAT LITTLE REMAINED of Derby and the surrounding county after 1071 was passed by William the Bastard to Henri de Ferrers. Henri was one of dozens of close friends who had sailed over from Normandy with William to conquer England. This particular slice of the cake cannot have been very appealing following the King's ethnic cleansing policy, but Henri gamely set up shop at Tutbury, just over the border in Staffordshire.

It was Henri's grandson Robert who was first given the Earl of Derby title, in 1138, after raising an enormous blood-thirsty army, of the kind not seen since the days of the Vikings, to repel an invasion by the Scottish King David. With other Midland and north England Norman nobles and their conscripts, he marched to Northallerton in Yorkshire and forced the Scots back over the border.

The King of England at that time was Étienne de Blois, commonly Anglicised to 'Stephen'. He was in France when David invaded, and, given that his reign ushered in a period of nationwide civil war and anarchy that turned England into a kind of 'Harrying of the North' theme park, most of the Anglo-Normans were happy to see the back of him. But no matter how much they hated Étienne, an invasion was

King Stephen.

an invasion, and David had to be dealt with. De Ferrers quickly sent him packing, leaving corpses scattered all the way up to the border.

Upon his return, Étienne de Blois was so impressed by Robert's efficiency and stout-heartedness that he created the Earl of Derby title. The document that accompanied it did not hang on Robert's wall for long, though, as he died the following year, possibly from illness resulting from his war wounds.

TARNISHED TITLE

The English did not take up arms against the Norman domination in Derbyshire, and Derby folk remained quietly industrious and pragmatic, much like the mild-mannered Britons that had lived here at the time of the Roman invasion. The Earls of Derby grew stronger as the years passed, erecting manors and churches and riding high in the feudal stakes – notably when Robert's grandson William married Margaret Peverel, last surviving heir of one of Derbyshire's other powerful Norman families, and from whom he inherited a huge amount of property and income, including a cash-in-hand sum from every toll, trial, fine, forfeiture and extortion that occurred on his patch.

William took part in a rebellion against incumbent King Henry II, and civil war was still ongoing when Henry's son Richard the Lionheart came to the throne. The revolting nobles were eventually defeated, and Richard stripped William de Ferrers of all his titles, giving the Earl of Derby tag to his own brother John (of Magna Carta fame). But, as eighteenth-century chronicler William Hutton put it, after John himself became King, 'the lustre of the title, like a candle in the sun, was lost in that of the Crown.'

King John gave the Earl of Derby title back to William's son, another William,

along with much of the property and income associated with its glory days. William was even Sheriff of Nottingham for seven weeks in 1194.

CHARIOT-TEARS

William's son, yet another William, reaped the rewards, but met a violent and possibly unique death for a thirteenth-century man. He suffered terrible gout (a curse that afflicted many of the de Ferrers), which prevented him from walking. Instead, according to Victorian historians, he chose to travel by chariot, and on one such jaunt he was dislodged from the passenger seat when his charioteer took a bend at speed. It was Britain's first chariot-related death since Boadicea's day (a colourful notion foiled by a rival claim, that he was being carried on a litter – a carriage-like box borne by human rather than animal muscle – which is much less exciting).

William's fifteen-year-old son Robert took the title in 1254, along with a huge amount of debt; and once into adulthood he joined the Second Barons' War against Henry III, under Simon de Montfort. Taking an army from Derby and elsewhere, he attacked royal stronghold Worcester, ransacking the Jewish quarter, plundering every private or religious establishment he could find, damaging the royal park; and, most importantly, seizing and burning the bonds which recorded his various debts.

The Derby men who had joined Robert de Ferrers' army were the lucky ones. Those left behind bore the brunt of the King's revenge when he sent his ruthless son (later Edward I) to burn the Earl's estates and put any bystander to the sword. For the second time since the Norman Conquest, poor Derby and its docile occupants were crushed.

Above   *King
John signing the Magna Carta.*

Below   *Henry III, who put Derby to the sword
(left) and Edward I (right), who burnt de Ferrers'
estates.*

'Wicked' King John, holding the
Magna Carta; he gave the de
Ferrers family back their titles.
He is best remembered, however,
as the enemy of English legend
Robin Hood.

DE FERRERS GETS THE SACK

When the rebellion died down, Robert, having fallen out with de Montfort, arranged to pay for a royal pardon. Then, when the heat was off, he raised another army from his bases in Derby and Duffield, refused to pay the agreed sum to the King, and in 1266 tried to rekindle the civil war. By this time, Simon de Montfort was dead. Henry III sent an army to poor Derby once again, and the townsfolk must have been very relieved when its Earl surrendered without too much bloodshed: he was caught hiding under some sacks of wool in one of the city's churches. He was imprisoned, and his vast lands and titles were passed to the King's unpromisingly named second son, Edmund 'Crouch-back'.

After three years in the nick, Robert somehow managed to persuade Edmund that, on receipt of £50,000, he should let the land and titles revert to him. Robert didn't have £5, never mind £50,000, but he managed to get securities from an impressive cast of aristocrats. It was all hot air, though: the money was never paid, and de Ferrers regained none of his titles, just a small part of his former kingdom at Chartley in Staffordshire. He died in 1279, and with him faded what had been one of the country's most powerful families.

DE MONTFORT: SIMON SAYS 'WAR!'

*   French by birth, Simon de Montfort shared a great grandparent with, and married the sister of, Henry III.

*   He became Earl of Leicester in 1239.

*   In that same year he fell out with Henry III, and let off steam by joining the Crusades and spending time in France.

*   He became the focus point for all disaffected English noblemen in the 1260s.

*   His successes in the Second Barons' War, 1263–4, made him the effective ruler of England.

*   He called the first directly elected parliament in medieval Europe in 1265, with voting rights for all men who owned the freehold of land earning rent of 40 shillings or more annually. His aim was a new, more democratic system, based on a constitution.

*   The King's forces replied in that same year by defeating and dismembering de Montfort at the Battle of Evesham.

1322

ROBERT DE HOLLAND'S INVISIBLE ARMY

PLAYING A KEY part in King Edward I's wars against William Wallace and Scotland, Robert de Holland rose to lofty heights in Derbyshire. In 1307 he was granted swathes of land that had once belonged to the Earls of Derby, including manors at Osmaston and Normanton in what is now the south of Derby, and neighbouring estates including Chellaston, Swarkestone and Melbourne. In the latter he transformed the manor house into the stone fortress of Melbourne Castle, after receiving from the Crown the much-coveted 'licence to crenellate' in 1311.

Robert was now the most powerful man in Derbyshire, but the land came at a price: he was ordered to march back to Scotland to fight the forces of Robert the Bruce. But de Holland's gory glory years were behind him: Scotland was in the ascendancy, Edward I died in that same year (1307), and new King Edward II did not inspire the same martial instincts as his father.

Edward II still favoured Robert de Holland. He made him a baron in 1315, and welcomed him into his inner circle of favourites. Robert was keen to keep the land and titles, but his loyalties lay not with the King but rather with his former lord and mentor Thomas, Earl of Lancaster and Derby. Lancaster hated the King, particularly despising his court favourite (and lover) Piers Gaveston: Gaveston was famous for his jokes about the court, mocking Lancaster's style of walking, and calling the Earl of Warwick 'the black dog of the Ardenne Forest' because of his dark colouring. He was to regret saying it – Warwick carried him off to his castle, where his head was swiftly chopped off. Lancaster watched with glee at his execution.

A GOOD HIDING

King Edward now hated Lancaster above all others. In 1322, Lancaster led likeminded barons, including Robert de Holland, in an armed rebellion. Not wishing to fall completely from royal favour, however, Robert dragged his feet and failed to produce the troops he promised. Lancaster was not impressed, but de Holland assured him that the army had indeed been mustered. It was time for the big push.

The Earl of Lancaster, now in alliance with his former enemy Robert the Bruce, prepared for battle in the Midlands. Robert de Holland was still promising Derby's support, and all the troops were ready for action. But when the King's

THE PEASANTS ARE REVOLTING!

The years around 1314 were some of the most horrible in English history.

*   Thousands of Englishmen died at the disastrous Battle of Bannockburn.
*   Thousands more died of epidemics in these years: there were so many corpses around that it was impossible to bury them all.
*   Famine struck after the harvest failed several years in a row (rotted, it is said, by enormous storms that swept the country). Food grew so scarce that dogs, cats and rats were eaten, and it was rumoured that prisoners in the country's jails were killing and eating each other. Dead bodies were being put into the pot, and babies had to be carefully hidden to stop them being stolen and eaten.
*   Sheep died of 'the rot', and cattle and pigs died of starvation in their hundreds.
*   As prices rose, Britain's wealthy lords sacked all their servants to save money. The unemployed formed into great gangs, roaming the countryside looking for people to rob. These desperate mobs lingered for years afterwards.
*   A tanner's son from Exeter called John Poydras, spurred on by Edward II's unpopularity, spread a rumour that *he* was the real son of Edward I, and that he had been stolen from his cradle by a wicked nurse and replaced with baby Edward. Eventually arrested, he claimed that he had been told to say all this by a Devil that lived in his house, disguised as a cat. He was executed shortly afterwards.

Lancaster receives Gaveston's severed head; Piers once mocked the Earl's way of walking, earning his hatred. Lancaster watched with delight as the axe fell.

army crossed the River Trent, de Holland was suddenly nowhere to be seen. He had abandoned Lancaster at this crucial moment and crossed over to the King's side, holing himself up in Derby just in case everything went wrong. Lancaster, with several thousand men less than he had hoped, retreated to Boroughbridge in Yorkshire, where nemesis awaited him. He was defeated, captured, humiliated and executed: he went to his death in shabby clothes upon a weedy and mangy horse, with a hood over his head, and was beheaded by the public executioner. Robert de Holland then emerged from hiding in Derby and surrendered to the King, pointing out that he had swapped

Edward III, whose formidable military prowess is reflected by the suit of armour and sword that he wears.

Edward II. The poker-shaped sceptre he is holding is unfortunately rather fitting – legend has it that he was killed by the application of just such a wand, red hot, to the royal anus, at Berkeley Castle in Gloucestershire.

sides and not lifted a finger against the Crown.

Edward II was not impressed, however. He suspected that de Holland was still loyal to Lancaster's rebellious aims, and took him from Derby in chains to languish in Dover Castle prison. Although he was pardoned by Edward II's successor Edward III in 1327, he still had the Earl of Lancaster, in the guise of Thomas' brother Henry, to contend with. Before he could lock himself in the highest crenellated tower of Melbourne Castle, he was captured, condemned as a traitor and executed. His severed head was delivered to Henry; his body was buried in Lancashire.

MELBOURNE CASTLE: LICENCE TO CRENELLATE

*   Rather like James Bond's Licence to Kill, these were issued only to trusted individuals. Under Norman rule you couldn't build a castle – i.e. 'crenellate' – without one of these prized documents.

*   Unlicenced castles were still fairly common, however (1,115 of them in the rocky years of the mid-twelfth century), and were usually an outward sign of defiance against the Crown.

*   The idea was that private fortifications should be limited to those barons who supported the monarch, to avoid painful sieges in the all-too-common event of civil war.

*   The first licence was given in the 1120s; Edward III (Robert de Holland's pardoner) issued 181, but the fad then went into decline, and during the reign of Edward IV (1442–83) only three were issued.

*   Melbourne Castle's crenellations were carried out 1313–14, at a colossal cost of £1,314. The building reverted to the Crown in 1327 after Robert de Holland fell from favour, and was demolished in 1637 so that its once proud stones could be used elsewhere.

RESURRECTION AT BOSWORTH FIELD

THE TITLE 'EARL of Derby' had not been in use since the disgrace and death of its last holder, Robert de Ferrers, in 1279. But sixty years later, Edward III resurrected it and bestowed it on Henry Plantagenet, son of Henry, Earl of Lancaster, who had grabbed large chunks of Derby and the surrounding county following the execution of Robert de Holland.

The title passed, via his daughter Blanche, to 1st Duke of Lancaster, John of Gaunt, when the two married. John was remembered locally for bringing the bloody spectacle of bull-running to England, with annual bouts between the men of Derbyshire and Staffordshire. He was a son of Edward III, and effective ruler of England during the minority rule of Richard II. This was the loftiest height to which the Earl of Derby title ever reached; its next holder, Gaunt and Blanche's son Henry Bolingbroke, nearly took Derby all the way to the throne as Henry IV, in 1399, after winning the latest rounds of civil war and allegedly having King Richard II murdered – but he ditched the Earl tag before assuming the Crown.

After this, no Earl of Derby darkened the pages of history until 1485, and the Battle of Bosworth Field.

The murder of Richard II – an Earl of Derby was rumoured to be behind this brutal attack.

GAUNT'S GAME OF BULL-RUNNING

* John of Gaunt was a well-travelled man, and during his holidays in Spain he had witnessed bull-running of the type still observed in modern day Pamplona. Determined to introduce the quaint old blood sport to England, he instigated the Tutbury bull-running, which occurred every August.

* Robin Hood is said to have married in Tutbury during the bull-running feast.

* Prior to the bull run, the Tutbury beast had its tail and ears lopped off, its body soaped, and its nose stuffed with ground pepper to put it in a suitably murderous mood.

* In its latter years, the event was a contest between the men of Tutbury and their neighbours over the border in Derbyshire. The bull ran through the streets with young men in hot pursuit, attempting to cut a strip of skin from the animal; and if the Derbyshire contingent managed to drive it over the River Dove into their home county, the beast was theirs.

* Many travelled from Derby and Ashbourne to pursue the Tutbury bull. Ashbourne had its own popular annual bull-baiting too, which survived into the nineteenth century.

* In some parts of the county, bylaws said that bulls *had* to be baited before butchering, to tenderise the meat.

* A fatal goring (not the first) brought the Tutbury tradition to an end in 1777.

CROWNING ACHIEVEMENT

In the late fifteenth century, George Stanley was thrown into prison by Richard III to make sure George's father, Thomas, behaved. Thomas had won fame as a soldier under Edward IV, fighting against Scotland, but Richard III distrusted him.

Initially Richard attempted to have Thomas Stanley, who became the 1st Earl of Derby when the title was revived, assassinated, but he then changed tack, aware of the loyalty the Stanley name inspired. He instead promoted him to Steward of the Household and Lord High Constable of England. It was an uneasy alliance, with a bloody end: in 1485, the Stanleys abandoned Richard III on the battlefield at Bosworth Field, and the betrayed King charged to his death, allegedly crying, 'Treason, treason, treason!' as he went. It was Thomas Stanley who took the crown from the corpse of Richard III, and placed it on the head of Henry Tudor, Duke of Lancaster, who promptly became Henry VII.

Richard II.

Clockwise from above:

John of Gaunt, who brought the gruesome game of bull-running to England.

Richard III: the crown was lifted from his bloody head – or from a nearby thorn bush, according to the legend – and placed on the head of the new King by Thomas Stanley, 1st Earl of Derby.

Charles I, who sent Stanley's descendant into Bolton, where he massacred 1,000 prisoners.

The resurrected Earldom of Derby was presented to him as a gift of thanks. The body of Richard was carried, naked, from the field of battle and slung over a horse like a hunting trophy. It was carried in this manner all the way to Leicester, dripping mud and blood as it went.

Thomas died in 1504; George never quite recovered from his ordeal in prison and passed away in 1488. The title fell to George's son Thomas, and then went from father to son for several generations. The most notable achievement of the Earls in the sixteenth century is the fact that successive title holders Edward, Henry, Ferdinando and William (died 1642) managed to live through and curry favour with all the Tudors – murderous Henry VIII, doomed young Edward VI, Bloody Mary I, and the grotesquely fickle Elizabeth I – and out the other side into the Stuart era.

ANOTHER FINE MESS, STANLEY

Successor James Stanley did not do so well, however. He managed to rise to the top of the Royalist heap under Charles I, and ordered the executions of 1,000 prisoners in Bolton during the Civil War – remembered in history as 'the Bolton Massacre'. In his last battle, near Wigan, he was said to have gained seven musket-shot holes on his breast-plate, thirteen sword-blows on his bent helmet, five wounds on his body, with two horses killed under him.

The Earl of Derby was eventually captured (after escaping once from his prison in Chester by climbing down the walls on a rope), and was beheaded outside a pub in Bolton on 15 October 1651. He had waited for three hours inside the building beforehand, whilst his executioners erected the platform and block upon which he would receive the chop.

1556

WHAT A WASTE!

IN THE SIXTEENTH century, wise men and women kept their heads down in order to keep them on their shoulders. When Edward VI was succeeded by Catholic firebrand 'Bloody' Mary I in 1553, yesterday's cleric was today's potential firelighter.

One of the most unlikely victims of the denominational merry-go-round was Joan Waste of Derby, a 'poor honest godlie woman', according to an account published seven years after her death. One of twins, she was born blind in 1534, and soon learnt her surgeon-barber father William's sideline skills of ropemaking and stitching.

Joan was a devout Protestant, enjoying the fact that she could attend St Peter's Church in Derby and hear the service in English: the contemporary report says that 'by hearing homilies and sermons she became marvellously well affected to the religion then taught'. Her parents died when she was in her late teens, after which she lived with her twin, Roger.

ALL CHANGE!

One morning in 1553, Joan went to church and couldn't understand a word that was being said. Overnight, the clerics had reverted to Latin – and she was not pleased about it.

Joan had purchased a copy of the Bible in English during the previous reign, and this was a book that, under Queen Mary, represented a one-way ticket to prison. In the early days, Joan established an odd relationship with seventy-year-old John Hurt, a prisoner in the Common Hall of Derby. Joan asked him if he would read to her and, with far too much time and solitude on his hands, John became her talking book.

Whenever he was ill or otherwise engaged in his duties as a contrite prisoner, Joan looked for someone else to fulfil the role. Not everyone was as willing as John Hurt, but Joan was pragmatic. She would offer a small sum for the reading sessions, informing the reader beforehand how many chapters she expected for her paltry pennies, and whether she required any passage to be repeated. By these means she acquired profound ecclesiastical knowledge, and was able to recite passages and argue against many of the perceived abuses performed by the church when judged against the word of the scriptures.

EATING FLESH AND DRINKING BLOOD – OR NOT

This was dangerous enough for a Protestant woman under a Protestant

Portrait of 'Bloody' Mary.

mere symbols of the flesh and blood of Christ, rather than the real thing. This was the detail that sent many of Queen Mary's 280-odd victims to the stake. In her response to the accusations, Joan cited other English devouts who had died for the Protestant faith. She said it was a simple question of belief in the truth, and that if her accusers believed there was no argument to be made beyond the obvious Catholic versus Protestant accusations, then (according to *Foxe's Book of Martyrs*) 'she desired them for God's sake not to trouble her, being a blind, poor and unlearned woman, with any further talk, saying (by God's assistance) that she was ready to yield up her life in that faith in such sort as they should appoint'.

The Bishop then pointed out that 'such sort as they should appoint' would involve torture and an excruciatingly painful death, and this had the desired effect on Joan. She asked him if he could swear on his conscience that the Catholic belief system was true, and that he would answer for poor Joan Waste at the Day of Judgement. Bishop Bane declared that he would, but was immediately advised by his chancellor, Dr Draycot, that he could not promise to argue before God for a heretic. In a classic game of good cop/bad cop, a much sterner voice now demanded that Joan either recant her heresies or burn. She repeated that unless they could openly state that their version of religion was God's own truth, rather than just a legal requirement, there was nothing more to be said. Like modern politicians avoiding the question, they failed to give her a yes/no answer.

BURNING ISSUES

Joan was imprisoned, and a month later the 'She's a Heretic!' documentation came through. She was made to attend All Saints' church in Derby, where a sermon

regime, but when the Catholics swept back to power, it was suicide. Joan made no secret of her prized English Bible, nor of her uncompromising views, and the newly Catholic state was soon knocking on her door. She was questioned both at home and in prison by Derby bailiffs, all acting for local Diocese boss Bishop Ralph Bane and his chancellor, Dr Anthony Draycot. Martyrdom as a religious heretic was now just a few bouts of legal pontificating away.

The chief accusation was that Joan refused to believe in transubstantiation – i.e. she maintained the Protestant line that the bread and wine of the Mass were

WHY BURN HERETICS?
A GUIDE FOR POTENTIAL BONFIRE BUILDERS

* Burning ensures that no blood is spilt, something which ensures that there is no blood on your hands.

* With the body consumed by fire, the heretic will have no body to accompany their soul into the afterlife following Judgement Day.

* Burning also cleanses the soul: in some cases this will ease the passage through the fires of Purgatory; although for heretics who are condemned to 'burn forever', this does seems a little counter-productive.

* Authorities should choose market days and public places, to ensure a good crowd.

* Supporters of the condemned may attend and assist, but should be flogged in the event of vocal demonstrations.

* Keep your faggots dry: if the fuel is damp the victim can take more than an hour to die, which is not good from an entertainment point of view.

* Bags of gunpowder may be tied to the victim at your discretion to speed up the process.

was preached by Dr Draycot against her heresies. This edifying lecture declared that she would burn at the stake, and then burn in Hell forever, and that no one was allowed to pray for her damned soul.

The first bit was certainly true. Twenty-two-year-old Joan Waste was taken to Windmill Hill Pit (on Lime Avenue, just off Derby's Burton Road), holding the hand of her twin Roger for as long as she and he were able. She asked the townsfolk to pray for her, and was then hoisted over the flames by a rope which, upon burning through, deposited her into the bonfire, on 1 August 1556. It is said that Dr Draycot, reflecting on his part in the death of an innocent, drowned his sorrows with lunch at an inn and slept through the execution. His own imprisonment and death through illness came under the next monarch, Protestant Queen Elizabeth I.

Windmill Hill Pit in Derby is now the site of St Joseph's Roman Catholic Church, which may or may not be appropriate, depending how you look at it.

Queen Elizabeth I: she had the priest who sent Joan to her death imprisoned.

1588

THERE'S A PRIEST IN MY CHIMNEY

ON 24 JULY 1588 three Roman Catholic priests, Nicholas Garlick, Robert Ludlam and Richard Simpson, were hanged, drawn and quartered in public in Derby.

Garlick and Ludlam, both Derbyshire men, had trained for the priesthood in France, and priests schooled in Catholic countries were not even supposed to set foot on English soil; but these were early days for English Protestantism, and the country still had many powerful 'recusant' nobles who secretly practised the old religion – and to practice the religion, you needed ordained priests, otherwise there could be no Mass. Amongst these recusants was John Fitzherbert of Padley Manor in Derbyshire, brother of Sir Thomas Fitzherbert (Lord of Norbury, Padley and several other Derbyshire acres besides). The two young priests lodged with him.

Greed-fuelled betrayal soon scuppered them all, however. John's son, another Thomas, coveted the family land and titles, most of which belonged to his Uncle Thomas, who had been in prison for religious reasons since 1561. He alerted the thought police to the illegal deeds of his father, and although the authorities appear to have known all about the Fitzherberts' Catholic tastes, they could not ignore his son's accusations. Young Thomas told

chief priest-catcher and Privy Councillor Richard Topliffe exactly when his father would be at home, offering £3,000 as a sweetener, and on 12 July 1588 the police raided Padley Manor. They not only collared John, but also discovered two young illegal immigrant priests hiding in the chimney.

WHERE THERE'S A WILL, THERE'S A WAY

The threesome were slung into the back of the police wagon and deposited in the bowels of Derby Gaol, where they were suddenly neighbours to John's brother Sir Thomas. As the owner of all the Fitzherbert lands, including Padley, where John had been living since his sibling's incarceration, Thomas senior quickly revised his will to disinherit his treacherous nephew. Richard Topliffe managed to intercept the will, however, and assigned to himself the plum property at Padley, allowing Thomas junior to take Norbury. John and Thomas senior eventually died in prison.

Also languishing in Derby Gaol at this time was Sheffield-born priest Richard Simpson, destined to become the third martyr, along with Garlick and Ludlam.

St Mary's Bridge, where the men were executed. (Photograph with kind permission of Andy Savage, www.derbyphotos.co.uk)

He had done a previous spell in gaol at York, and had later committed covert Catholic things in Lancashire and the Peak District area of Derbyshire, until one of his flock revealed himself as a spy and handed Simpson to the Protestant authorities early in 1588. Torture and solitude broke him, and he had agreed to take on board the Protestant argument, as a result of which his death sentence was put on hold. However, the arrival of the still-zealous Garlick and Ludlam firmed his resolve, and the three now prepared themselves for martyrdom.

SAINTS' CLUB: DISMEMBERS ONLY

At the trial, on 23 July 1588, Nicholas Garlick became the triumvirate's spokesman. He argued that he had returned to England 'not to seduce but to induce' people to return to the Catholic fold. It all fell on deaf ears, of course, forcing him to give the memorable parting shot: 'Cain would never be satisfied until he had the blood of Abel!'

On the following day, the three men were dragged on hurdles to the place of execution at St Mary's Bridge. En route, one of the crowd shouted out to Nicholas Garlick that he was a friend, and that as children they had gone on shooting trips together; to which the condemned man replied, 'True, but now I am to shoot such a shot as I never shot in all my life!'

Garlick was the first of the three to be strung up. He was wearing a doublet (a tight jacket) and after he was taken from the rope this had to be removed. Unfortunately, he revived at this point, and eyewitnesses said he spoke to the executioners before having his genitals sliced off, his bowels pulled out and burnt, and his body dismembered.

Simpson was next, and was said to be calm, almost cheerful. Ludlam had the unenviable task of following the other two, having witnessed their messy demise. He offered up prayers for his soul, for England, for the crowd and for those who had brought him to this sorry state.

After the gore-fest was over, chunks of corpse were displayed at the St Mary's Bridge execution site, and the three heads, on poles, were placed at different spots around the town – and, according to some accounts, were taken on a 'Let this be a warning' tour of Derbyshire too. But eventually they were rescued by Catholic sympathisers and buried.

The road to saintdom is a long one, and the three men had to wait until 1888 to be declared venerable – the precursor to full sainthood – and were finally beatified by Pope John Paul II in 1987, becoming fully fledged saints, 'the Blessed Padley Martyrs'.

YOU SAY 'TO MARTYR'...

Dying as a Catholic martyr was not as easy as you might think. Roman Catholic policy against England meant that, in English law, anyone supporting the Pope was a traitor, and could therefore be executed for treason. Which is not the same as being executed as a martyr.

In 1587, the Pope named William Allen (founder of Catholic colleges in Flanders and Rome) Cardinal of England, the first such title since Henry VIII's Reformation. This had infuriated Queen Elizabeth, and any condemned Catholic would have to deny the authority of Cardinal Allen if he or she wished to die as a martyr rather than a mere traitor.

The only way around this conundrum was to profess yourself an unrepentant Catholic with the salvation of England as your goal, whilst condemning the Pope's edicts and refusing to recognise Allen's authority in England.

It was a fine line to tread, for if you were disloyal to the Pope you couldn't be a practicing Roman Catholic, but it was just about manageable with some philosophical, evasive arguing.

1587–1932

ACTS OF GOD

PRIOR TO THE twentieth century, Derby was prone to regular flooding. Many lives were lost over the years, and the waters were directly responsible for rotting the timbers in various buildings, including the town's accident-prone churches.

One of the first recorded floods was in 1587, when rising waters swept away St Mary's Bridge and the mills that stood at the bottom of St Michael's Lane. At the beginning of the following century, St Werburgh's Church succumbed to the combined strife of water-induced rot from below and a structural engineering time-bomb above. On 2 January 1601 the tower, too heavy for its soggy supports, collapsed, taking much of the medieval church with it. It had been rebuilt by 1608, suffered more damage during the hurricane of 1662, and in 1698 the remaining medieval bits fell down.

St Peter's is the only ancient church in Derby that retains any of its original structure, all the others having followed the destructive path of St Werburgh's. In most cases it was a simple case of inaction in the face of the inevitable, the last major neglect-induced collapse taking place at St Michael's in 1856. In other cases, such as the various doomed buildings on the ring-road site once occupied by St Alkmund's, it was an even simpler case of wilful demolition.

CRIES FOR HELP DROWNED OUT

In 1610, Markeaton Brook rose after heavy rainfall and began to drain into the low-lying town gaol. Three prisoners unlucky enough to be resident at the time cried out for help, but their gaolers were too busy escaping to come to their aid. The cellmates drowned, and the brook repeated its performance the following year.

The year 1616 was a particularly bad era for weather. Records state that the calamities began on 14 May: 'There happened this year such a land flood from the brook that in the memory of man the like was never seen. There hastened a great drought, a great snow, and after that a great drought which continued four months.'

There was more heavy snow in 1634, killing four people caught with inappropriate clothing between Derby and Chaddesden. Drought dried up the riverbed of the Derwent in 1661, and the following year was visited by very fickle winds: 'A dreadful hurricane in Derby that blew up trees by the roots and did damage the south side of the town.' The north side was left unscathed, however: '...not a tile, scarce a straw stirred off any house.'

IT ALL COMES FLOODING BACK

Another flood in 1673 sought to do further damage to poor St Werburgh's. The Churchwarden's Account Book records breathlessly: 'July 19 1673. Being Sabbath Day at night there was a great flood of water was two foot high in the middle alley it were measured so that it came into chests and wet all the writings such a flood were not known in our age before. Cloves to sweeten the church after the flood – £0 0s 2d.' The cloves were meant to purify the air to counter the contagion associated with the sewer-filled water. Other herbs were used for this purpose too, including cinnamon, frankincense, juniper and tobacco; or, in the absence of these, humble charcoal.

The church was not the only building to suffer: the flood also 'filled the cellars as high as Rotten Row, and broke down three of ten bridges. St James's bridge was landed at the Sun inn, St Peter's Street.'

After yet another St Werburgh flood in 1687, plans were devised to make the edifice more watertight. That year's clean-up cost was one shilling and fourpence, and in 1691, as the rainy July season got underway, a further two pennies were spent blocking up the north door to keep out the floods. In 1696 the precautions were observed to have worked, that year's floodwater flowing safely around the sealed door. But two years later, the waters washed away the final bits of the original church. The defences failed again in 1715 and ninepence had to be spent 'for levelling the North Alley after the flood'.

YOU'RE FIRED!

Fire has done its bit to shape Derby too, with two outbreaks in 1650 and 1675, miniature versions of London's more celebrated razing. Not much of the older, wooden parts of Derby survived these conflagrations. But the town's biggest blaze was in 1340 when Spondon – a separate settlement back then – was reduced to ashes by what locals called the Great Fire of Spondon. It began in a malt house and was aided by ferocious winds. With Spondon all but gone, villagers petitioned King Edward III, and he generously granted them exemption from parish taxes for nine months. The money they saved enabled them to embark on a new building project, although this medieval episode of *Grand Designs* took fifty years to complete.

With most of the wooden buildings gone, and stricter fire regulations in place following the burning down of the town hall in 1841, by the twentieth century only the ever-overflowing Derwent and Markeaton Brook were left to bring regular Acts of God to Derby. On 22 May 1932, water made its last major assault on the town, drowning the city centre in several feet of good old-fashioned muddy flood. In the aftermath, the corporation finally spent the necessary time, money and expertise to sort out the problem via improved drainage, culverts and defences, most notably the Derwent flood barrier.

Besides, in the modern city of Derby, where redundant St Werburgh's church is used for commercial purposes and the remaining chunk of Darley Abbey is a pub, it is not surprising that Acts of God have ground to a halt.

DERBY GAOL: EN-SUITE CELLS WITH RUNNING WATER

* In 1166 Derby was instructed to build a gaol, an order which it took over three and a half centuries to comply with.
* The town gaol was eventually built in 1532 by order of King Henry VIII – prior to that, local prisoners had been carted off to the cells at Nottingham Castle.
* The appropriately squalid prison was located at Cornmarket on the banks of the ever-flooding Markeaton Brook: the gaoler's quarters were at street level, but the cells were below ground.
* Markeaton Brook doubled as the town sewer, and so even when not flooded the gaol was particularly foul.
* In 1755 Derby discussed plans for a new gaol, one that would punish its inmates without exposing them to the knee-deep sewage and attendant diseases of the old institution.
* The site chosen for the new gaol was Nun's Green – appropriate given that this was where one of Derby's gallows was erected. Much of the old building was used in the construction of the new.

The Cornmarket, Derby, at the end of the nineteenth century. In 1532, the prison was located here.

Above   *A dramatic rendering of the Great Fire of Spondon, which reduced this area of the town – then a separate township – to ashes.*

Below   *The River Derwent, cause of many of Derby's disasters. (Library of Congress, Prints & Photographs Division, LC-DIG-ppmsc-0828)*

UNCIVIL WAR: SIR JOHN GELL, GOVERNOR OF DERBY

CHARLES I SPENT his entire reign looking for ways to raise money. One of his early methods of raking in the cash was a levy known as Ship Money, and in 1635, Derby – and the surrounding county – was assessed for the first time. A new breed of tax collectors was unleashed, demanding £175 from the city. No tax is ever popular, but to landlocked Derby the notion of forking out to finance ships seemed absurd. It was a brave man who knocked on the doors here and asked for contributions.

Derby's incarnations of this brave soul were High Sheriffs Sir John Gell of Hopton (near Wirksworth) and his brother-in-law, Sir John Curzon of Kedleston.

Gell, along with the Derby burghers who ran the town's finances, was very much on the King's side – to begin with. He was entertained in 1635 at the townhouse of William Cavendish, Earl of Devonshire, who was primed for the occasion by the town bigwigs with 'a fat ox, a calf, six fat sheep, and a purse of money, that he might keep hospitality in the town'. This did the trick, King Charles granting 'loyal' Derby a new charter in 1637, for a whacking great fee, by which a corporation was formed with Mayor, aldermen, burgesses and all the other trappings. The Mayor had to pay the Crown £70 a year for the privilege of receiving Derby's tolls.

But Derby – as ever – was more self-serving than loyal, and more pragmatic than heroic. Realising how badly business would suffer in a civil war, the townsfolk petitioned King and Parliament to settle their differences. When war loomed, and the King marched through Derby before setting the royal standard at Nottingham in August 1642, a call to arms for all good men, loyal and true, only twenty Derbeians followed him. The King then borrowed £300 from the new corporation (the smallest sum they could get away with), along with a modest haul of arms. Charles promised to return everything after the war. (Easier said than done if you lose the war, of course.)

TOWN HALL COUP

On 31 October 1642, former tax-collector Sir John Gell stepped into the spotlight in a new guise, informing the Mayor of Derby that he was bringing the army into the town on behalf of Parliament, with the town hall as their headquarters. He was, in fact, taking over the running of the city and imposing martial law. He was

DEAD LOSS

—⚬⚬⚬—

Sir John Gell and his men made an unorthodox coup after the Battle of Hopton Heath in Staffordshire on 19 March 1643. The conflict had ended in stalemate, Gell's Parliamentarians with the cold, dead corpse of the Royalist General Northampton, and the Royalists with the eight pieces of key enemy artillery.

Gell was keen to get the weaponry back, and hatched a bizarre plan. Taking Northampton's body back to Derby, he had it embalmed, and then ransomed it. Only if the King returned his weapons would he return the Earl.

The bait was not taken, and Northampton was later buried at All Saints' (now the cathedral) in the town. Lowering his expectations, Gell insisted that he should be compensated for the expense of embalming the corpse. That demand was ignored too.

—⚬⚬⚬—

to remain in this position, as Governor of Derby, for four years.

Gell did not trust the men of Derby, most of whom he suspected of being Royalist sympathisers, and locals did not take kindly to his appropriating and distributing the town's income as he saw fit – i.e. mainly to keep the army from mutineering. From his base at 16 Friar Gate he ruled the pro-Parliamentarian roost, gathering not just town money, but the income of seized Royalist estates too.

THE SIEGE OF DERBY...
ANY MOMENT NOW

One of John Gell's chief enemies was William Cavendish. Fear of potential attacks by Cavendish led Gell to install a permanent watch at the top of All Saints' church. Derbeians and men from the surrounding countryside were conscripted to build defences in preparation for a siege, with iron gates, defensive earthworks and a gunpowder mill. The atmosphere was not a happy one, and many men deserted both town and army. Not that the Derby army was a *total* waste of time. They had served under General Pointz at Stoke,

losing four men and all their horses, and being highly praised by the general for their bravery. Pointz also led them to victory, storming Royalist Belvoir Castle, and was so impressed by their valour that he persuaded Parliament to award them £40 to spend on drink back in Derby.

Gell also had an impressive military history behind him. He had led his troops to victory at Lichfield, Staffordshire, in 1643, and played a key role in the Battle of Hopton Heath almost immediately afterwards. No one could decide who had actually won this battle, but during it Gell was wounded in the neck (his doublet, with a hole in the neck, went on display in Hopton shortly afterwards). The fighting was so fierce that when the troops ran out of bullets, they turned their guns around and used them as clubs. The Royalists captured eight guns, but lost their commander, the Earl of Northampton, when they charged – his horse was shot out from under him before he was finished off. His body was stripped and robbed, and left naked in the dirt.

What John Gell now needed was a bloody battle in Derby, from which he could emerge triumphant. But, in spite of Cavendish and other Royalist hosts simmering on the borders, and in spite

TOP TEN GRIPES UNDER GOVERNOR JOHN GELL

* Citizens were expected to donate their silver plate, to be melted down and turned into coins to pay the army.
* Gell refused, initially, to employ members of the Derby Corporation.
* Oppression, as ever, fostered extremism: Puritan zealots such as Major Thomas Sanders of Cauldwell Hall and his magistrate sidekick, Gervase Bennet, were able to rise to power.
* The result was an awkward coalition: the Parliamentarian hierarchy insisted that Gell give Sanders a role, along with aggrieved locals such as Robert Mellor, son of the first Mayor, all of whom hated the Governor.
* Gell said that he would rather fight Sanders than any of his Royalist enemies, which was not very good for morale.
* In April 1644, Derby resident Catherine Gower was accidentally shot in the head and killed by one of the garrisoned soldiers.
* Officers in the Derby troop complained that they were not paid and that Gell was lining his own pockets with the melted-down silver.
* Townsfolk were compelled to work, unpaid, in fortifying the town.
* No financial records were kept, and decisions and finances seemed arbitrary.
* Laws were draconian, building on a pre-Gell precedent of 1639, when 'William Yates farted as he passed by Mr Mayor and was imprisoned for it'.

of engaging with the enemy elsewhere in the Midlands, the Derby attack never came.

SNATCHING DEFEAT FROM THE JAWS OF VICTORY

Summoned to fight with his forces at the crucial Battle of Naseby on 14 June 1645, Gell messed up the arrangements and failed to turn up. The Parliamentarians, under Oliver Cromwell and Sir Thomas Fairfax, crushed the Royalists nonetheless: Gell missed out on the glory and took all the flak. His next bad move came when he failed to apprehend the King during the Royalist retreat from Naseby towards Leicester, a procession he could easily have intercepted.

And that was that. Cromwell reordered his armed forces into the famous New Model Army, and flabby old regiments such as John Gell's were disbanded. Sir Thomas Fairfax came to Derby in person, staying for four days to oversee the redeployment of the garrison, quelling a mutiny when the army pointed out that Gell had not paid them. In September 1646, Gell was stripped of the Governor of Derby commission, and Mayor and burgesses assumed control once again.

John Gell, fleeing to London to escape Midlands' disgruntlement, was grilled by Parliamentary committees, with many complaints levelled at him by his former neighbours in Derby. But he managed to escape with no more than a stern telling off, and a three-year stint in the Tower of London a bit later as a result of his pro-Royalist views (having by now gone full circle in his loyalties). This was followed by a big thank you, accompanied by land and cash, when the monarchy was restored in 1660. So, against the odds, Sir John Gell got a happy ending.

AND CALL OFF CHRISTMAS!

AFTER THE DEPARTURE of its Parliamentarian garrison at the end of the Civil War in 1645, Derby emerged as a fully-fledged Puritan city. Well, on the surface at least. But what pro-Royalist passions lay simmering beneath?

The town's political wing was now led by two men who had been able to rise to prominence during the oppressive reign of Governor John Gell: Mayor Thomas Sanders of Cauldwell and Little Ireton, and Gervase Bennet, local justice. By the 1650s, these two had overseen the implementation of several Puritan party pieces, such as banning Christmas, exercising a policy of no-tolerance to all religious nonconformity, forbidding church wedding ceremonies in favour of civil ones, outlawing theatres and other entertainers, including Morris dancers, and advocating the grey religious austerity that gives the Commonwealth era such a bad name.

The last of Sir John Gell's cronies had lost their positions of power in the city by the end of Oliver Cromwell's stint as Lord Protector (although Gell's son John, wealthy from his investment in the lead-mining industry, sat for a Derbyshire seat in Parliament, as indeed did Mayor Thomas Sanders).

Oliver Cromwell, famous warts and all.

47

TEN THINGS THAT COULD GET YOU PUNISHED IN DERBY DURING THE COMMONWEALTH

Crime	Punishment
Swearing	Fine or imprisonment
Working on Sunday	The stocks
Going for a Sunday walk	Fine
Playing football	Whipping
Wearing makeup	On-the-spot fine and scrub
Wearing colourful clothes	Stocks or fine
Cooking Christmas dinner	Confiscation of dinner
Closing shop on Christmas Day	Fine
Being a Royalist	Imprisonment
Being a Catholic	Death

OUT WITH THE OLD, IN WITH THE HOPELESS

In 1658 Cromwell died, and his son Richard succeeded. This was a poor choice, as it smacked of the old monarchy, with its heirs and graces, and put a man with no military experience at the head of the New Model Army. Richard also had a colossal national debt to sort out, and seems to have lacked any natural aptitude. This, combined with the regime's loosening grip on the makeup of Parliament and the rise of pro-Restoration MPs, doomed the apparently amiable thirty-two-year-old from the start.

In August 1659, a pro-Restoration colonel, Charles White, appeared in Derby with a troop of men, confident that he could gain more supporters for the King here. He was working in league with expelled MP Sir George Booth, who had issued a declaration earlier in the month stating that 'arms had been taken up in vindication of the freedom of Parliament, of the known laws, liberty and property'. Charles White was urging Derby men to join an armed rebellion against the Government of Richard Cromwell. The

Richard Cromwell signing his abdication.

declaration was formally proclaimed in the town Market Place, and this day, 12 August, became known in Derby as White's Friday.

The result was more violently enthusiastic than White and his backers could have hoped, showing that several years of imposed republicanism had not converted the town to the Puritan or Cromwellian creeds. A large host of men, encouraged by the eager cooperation of the town militia, took whatever horses and gear they could get their hands on, shut their houses and shops, and prepared for open rebellion.

Above *Market Place. From here rebellion was preached, freak shows held and blood sports made available for the more sanguinary Derby residents.*

Below *Charles II.*

CLOSE SHAVE FOR REBELS

While this was going on, Sir George Booth raised an army of 3,000 men and seized Chester. General John Lambert attacked and destroyed this army at Nantwich, and captured Sir George – who was trying to escape, disguised as a woman – a few days later: he was caught whilst trying to shave

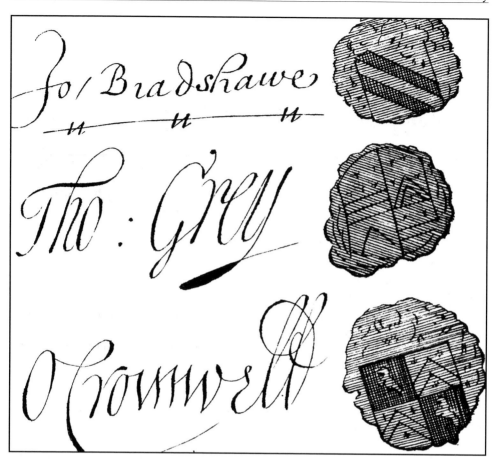

The signatures of Bradshawe and Cromwell on the death warrant of Charles I. A descendant of Bradshawe later suffered a horrible fate himself, having his head stoved in with a hammer by a servant girl he was attempting to rob.

at Newport Pagnell. Lambert then sent 250 cavalry to Derby to destroy the malcontents, but rebellion was defused before they reached the town by a few strategic arrests.

But in less than a year, Booth was not only out of prison, along with the Derby rebels, but back in Parliament. The Commonwealth had crumbled away, pro-Restoration MPs had banded together with the old school Royalists, and, after a decade of painful war, revolution, regicide and reform, the Parliamentary ruling that ushered in Charles II was bloodless.

Royalist civic business in Derby, instigated as recently as 1637 but rudely interrupted by civil war, could now continue. It was as if John Gell, Thomas Sanders and the Cromwells had never happened.

THREE MEN WALK INTO A COURT, AND OTHER GALLOWS HUMOUR

HORSE THEFT WAS a common offence in Derbyshire (second only to sheep stealing), and the Derby Assizes heard countless tales of how palfreys had been pilfered and steeds stolen. The most memorable of these occurred some time in the 1660s, when the judge entertained a spot of spontaneous malice to giddy-up the proceedings. Exact dates are elusive, which is always an indication that historians should have a large pinch of salt at hand.

So, somewhere on the borderlands of truth and myth, a man called Crosland was found guilty, along with his two sons, of stealing horses. The offence was not a capital one at the time, but that did not stop the Bench from having a bit of fun. The family of three were told that one of them could go free, if he agreed to hang the other two. This outrageous judgement was remembered for years to come, and indignant late eighteenth-century chronicler William Hutton was moved to declare, 'When power wantons in cruelty, it becomes detestable, and gives greater offence than even the culprits... Barbarous judges! I am sorry I cannot transmit their names to posterity.' (Lack of names is another alarm bell when searching for hard facts).

I SLAY, I SLAY, I SLAY...

Never can a job offer have had more strings, and ropes, attached. The proposition was put first to the horrified Crosland senior. 'Distress', as Hutton goes on to say, 'is the season for reflection'. Crosland replied: 'Was it ever known that a father hanged his children? How can I take away those lives which I have given, have cherished, and which, of all things, are most dear?' So saying, he declined the position, and the question went to the eldest son.

'Though life is the most valuable of all possessions, yet even *that* may be purchased too dear,' he replied. 'I cannot consent to preserve my existence by taking away him who gave it; nor could I face the world, or even myself, should I be left the only branch of that family which I had destroyed.' Hutton underlines this as containing 'love, tenderness, compassion, and all the appendages of honour'.

Finally, the question was put to John Crosland, the youngest. Would he hang his father and brother? Yes, and anyone else they cared to wheel in, replied John. He later carried out the dastardly deed with such cheery efficiency that the judge offered him the full-time job of executioner not just for Derby, but for 'two or three neighbouring counties'.

THE EXECUTIONER, THE MILLER, AND THE PUNCHLINE

The tale of John Crosland has all the hallmarks of an urban legend. Like many old tales and jokes, it involves three protagonists. 'The Miller of Derby', an eighteenth-century folk song, is in this category too. A dying miller asks his three sons in turn how they will carry on the business: 'If to you the mill I leave, pray tell me the toll that you'll receive?' – i.e. how much would each son take for himself from every sack of corn.

The first says that he'll take just a peck from each, and is dismissed by his indignant parent. The second says he will steal half the corn, but that is still not good enough. The third says he will steal the lot, and the father replies: 'Yes, you are a stout young blade! You've surely learned your father's trade, and when I'm dead and in decay, I know you won't fool my mill away!'

PROMOTION TO OFFICIAL BOGEY MAN

At a guinea a go, executioner was a well-paid job, and Crosland is said to have enjoyed his new role immensely. He even made sure that the hanged men were properly dead after they had been cut down from the gallows, although by what means Hutton is too coy to say. This was a macabre act of kindness, as hanged men had sometimes been known to reanimate.

The recorded speeches of the Croslands are probably inventions, the whole story smacking of urban legend – the only sure-fire fact is that John Crosland was Derby's chief executioner in the latter half of the seventeenth century. Like all men of his trade he was deeply unpopular, and this was probably sufficient to give rise to the courtroom tale; although it is still possible that he did actually meet his family members on the gallows at some point.

Well into the eighteenth century, mothers would use the infamous executioner, who died unrepentant in 1705, as a 'nursery bogie', warning their children that if they did not behave, 'John Crosland will come!' Hutton again: 'Loving none, and beloved by none, he spent a life of enmity with man. The very children pelted him in the streets. The mothers endeavoured to stop the infant cry with the name John Crosland; and I have the irksome task of recording him.'

1665

BURIED ALIVE

'THE PLAGUE' WAS an all too frequent visitor to England, and Derby did not miss out on its ravages. The disease has killed more inhabitants of the town than all the wars, riots and executions of this book combined.

The first bubonic flea in Derby probably hitchhiked on a batch of infested cloth in 1349, and from then on, in league with the black rat, it brought waves of death to the streets once or twice every generation, with the town's worst outbreaks occurring between 1586 and 1665. A nineteenth-century chronicler listed some of the worst years, from the safety of his post-plague era office in Derby:

*   1586 – 'The plague broke out in St Peter's parish.'
*   1592 – 'The plague again broke out in Derby, and great numbers were carried off by this awful calamity.'
    1636 – 'The spring was forward, and the plague again made its appearance; it was thought (first) in Bag lane.'
*   1665 – 'Derby was again visited with the plague; the town was forsaken; the farmers declined the Market Place, and grass grew upon the spot on which the necessaries of life had been sold. To prevent a famine, the inhabitants erected a stone a little way out of the town, for the purpose of exchange. This was called the Headless Cross.'

BUBONIC ANGEL

Edward Bennett, minister of All Saints', Derby, made the following stoical entry in the parish records in October 1593: 'About this tyme the plague of pestilence, by the great mercy and goodness of Almighty God, stayed past all expectation of man, for it ceased upon a sodayne, at which tyme it was dispersed in every corner of this whole p'she; there was not two houses together free from it, and yet the Lord bade the Angel stay as in Davide's tyme – hys name be blessed for ytt.'

All Saints' was where the plague had first broken out twelve months earlier, an area of town occupied largely by wealthy tradesmen, and 250 lives were lost.

The 1665 bout was England's last, and worst, outbreak. This was the year in which 'The Great Plague' ravaged Britain, bringing London to a standstill and putting poor Eyam in Derbyshire on the map as 'the Plague Village'. But although many historians describe Derby's sorry plight during that year, others maintain that the last outbreak in the town was actually in 1637.

Headless Cross. (Photograph with kind permission of Andy Savage, www.derbyphotos.co.uk)

One third of the town's population succumbed in 1665 (or 1637), and the majority of these were in the parish of St Peter's. It is said the bodies were packed into the graveyard vertically to accommodate the bubonic dead; and whether that's true or not, this was the most densely populated section of the city, and therefore prone to annihilation by any disease that happened to be around.

THE HORRORS OF THE PLAGUE!

Plague victims' symptoms were varied, and invariably horrid. Pus-filled, bleeding 'buboes' appeared around the lymph nodes in the armpits, groin and neck, accompanied by high fever and vomiting. Other types of boil and rash were recorded by the helpless doctors of the day too. One form of the disease infected the lungs, making breathing difficult and producing TB-like symptoms. Whatever the outward signs, 80 per cent of victims were dead within a week of infection.

Legend maintains that many of the bodies interred, sardine-like, at St Peter's were not actually dead at the time. One of the symptoms of the flea-borne disease was seizure, leading to a temporary coma, and in the haste to get suppurating corpses underground, mistakes were made. A few of these premature burial victims managed to claw their way out or kick open their coffins, while others simply screamed until they suffocated.

Even with these walking dead freeing up a bit of space in the cemetery, there was nowhere near enough room for everyone. Many bodies were buried at the town boundary – on Deadman's Lane, for example – and corpse pits abounded.

Clueless medics worked the Derby streets, dressed in bizarre masks and costumes, a combined body armour and

A PLAGUE UPON YOUR HOUSES!

———∞∞∞———

* The theory has been contested over the years, but current scientific thinking asserts that the various bouts of 'plague' and 'Black Death' in England were outbreaks of the still-extant disease known as bubonic plague.
* Bubonic plague is caused by the bacterium *Yersinia pestis*, which resides in the guts of fleas, which in turn suck up to rodents of various kinds, most notably the medieval era's *bête noire*, the black rat (*Rattus rattus*).
* The first *Yersinia pestis* to infest a flea's gut lived in China, its kindred travelling the Silk Road to reach Europe via the Crimea in 1346. Passenger ships and their rats transported the plague to every city on the map.
* Derby's 1665 death toll of between 30 and 40 per cent is a fair reflection of the general devastation across Europe, with even higher estimates of 60 per cent from some analysts. In terms of body count, Europe lost 100 million people between 1346 and 1400, with between 2 and 5 million in England.
* The economic and political chaos that came as a direct result of plague mortality has been blamed for most of the human upheavals of the 200 years following the first outbreak.
* Although 1665 was England's last outbreak, the plague did not die out in Europe until the nineteenth century.
* Modern antibiotics can reduce mortality rates to 1 per cent; but, if untreated, bubonic plague wipes out up to 90 per cent of its victims.

———∞∞∞———

herbal inhaler. Crosses were daubed on the doors of infected households, and barely a single residence in St Peter's escaped the dreaded paint.

HEADLESS CHICKENS

But somehow, in the midst of all this calamity, business in Derby had to continue. Fear shaped the market, and such trade as was possible took place on the edges of town – although, at the height of the plague in 1665, there was hardly anyone willing or able to trade, and so to add to the misery, the population faced starvation of the kind normally associated with long sieges.

Those who did choose to sell goods took precautions. Derby buyers were not allowed to touch anything before purchase, and the sellers disinfected their mouths with tobacco so as not to breathe in what they assumed was an airborne contagion.

This was based on the intriguing observation that the plague had never afflicted premises used by tobacconists.

Derby still has a relic of the plague years in the shape of the aforementioned Headless Cross, aka 'Vinegar Stone' or 'Plague Stone', at Friar Gate. It has a shallow depression at the top, which held the vinegar into which money was placed and disinfected during trading.

As a late eighteenth-century historian noted: 'A confidence, raised by necessity, took place between buyer and seller, which never existed before or since; the first could not examine the value of his purchase, nor the second that of his money.'

Derby commemorates the grim reality of plague with a couple of street names – in addition to the no-nonsense Dead Man's Lane, there is the less obvious Lousie Greaves Lane (originally 'Lousy Graves'), and possibly Blagreaves Lane, which may be a corruption of 'Black Graves Lane'.

I'LL HAVE TO PRESS YOU FOR AN ANSWER...

MOST CORPORAL **PUNISHMENT** in Derby involved a length of rope and a hangman. But there were other varieties too. Burning was a speciality for female religious heretics such as Joan Waste, but also for more homely heresies such as murdering their husbands or fathers. This was instead of the even more gruesome ordeal faced by most male heretics – hanging, drawing and quartering. It was deemed inappropriate to parade nude women in public, and nudity was a necessary part of the latter ordeal. Roasting women, on the other hand, was a spectacle acceptable for mass public consumption.

One speciality death, not actually intended as a form of execution but sometimes fulfilling the role anyway, occurred at Derby's Shire Hall, St Mary's Gate, on 14 March 1665, when a woman was 'pressed to death as a mute', in the words of William Hutton. This was the year of the Great Plague, which had perhaps put the judge in a particularly baleful frame of mind; but surely even in these dire circumstances, being a mute was not sufficient crime to merit such a terrible death? The story, scant in detail, offers few consolations for the soft hearted.

The most famous 'press yard' of them all: Newgate prison, London. A cart full of prisoners can be seen going to their deaths in the background.

HANGING ON HIS EVERY WORD...

Derby had started taking its executions seriously in 1534, when two gallows were erected for stringing up miscreants in full public view. Chronicler Francis White listed some of the highlights of the next 200 years in his 1857 history of Derbyshire:

* In 1590, one Okay was hanged in the Town Hall.
* In 1601, a woman was burnt to death, in Windmill Hill Pit, for poisoning her husband.
* In 1607, the witches of Bakewell were executed.
* In 1645, Richard Cockrum was executed on the gallows on Nun's Green, for killing a servant at the Angel.
* In 1705, John Crosland and his son were hanged for horse stealing (see the earlier story of the executioner).
* On 30 March 1738, Richard Woodward was hanged for highway robbery; he dressed himself in his shroud and walked to the place of execution.
* On 28 August 1740, George Ashmore was hanged for coining; the day after execution he was interred at Sutton-on-the-Hill, but his body was stolen by the resurrectionists. The 'resurrectionists' were followers of the trade of Burke and Hare, selling corpses to feed the boom in medical schools and dissections.

HANGED, DRAWN, QUARTERED, REPRIEVED

In 1681, Jesuit priest George Busby prepared to suffer the same fate as the Padley Martyrs. It was even the same date, so the omens were looking pretty bad.

During his trial at Derby's Shire Hall, Busby tried to prove that he was not born in England and therefore could not technically be called a traitor. The jury of local gentry, however, found him both English and guilty, and the judge passed a sentence that had not changed much since the martyrdom of Garlick, Ludlam and Simpson:

> ... conveyed thence on a hurdle to the place of execution, where you are to be hanged by the neck; that you be cut down alive, that your privy members be cut off, your bowels taken out and burnt in your view; that your head be severed from your body; that your body be divided into four quarters, which are to be disposed of at the King's pleasure; and God of his infinite mercy have mercy upon your soul.

But the judge, Mr Baron Street, having promised all this, then added one of Derby legal history's most comforting details: 'Though I must pass sentence upon you of course, the jury having found you guilty, yet I must tell you that his Majesty hath commanded me to reprieve you from execution.'

The woman, simply described as 'a deaf mute' in surviving records (hence the elusive nature of her name, presumably), was appearing on an unknown charge. When asked 'How do you plead?' she was, of course, unable to make any response. The judge asked her three times, and after three silences he was allowed to pass a 'judgement of penance'.

CRUSH DIET

Judgement of penance was meant to be a form of torture rather than execution, to force a reluctant accused criminal to plead one way or the other, and had been, for many years, an acceptable part of common law. The same legal system also said that if the accused died under torture, having 'stood mute' throughout – i.e. not entered a plea – their property and interests would be passed to their heirs rather than the Crown, so there was an incentive for the authorities to, literally, press for an answer.

In the 1665 Derby case, no amount of pressure was going to perform the miracle of making a dumb woman talk. But the judge was pedantic to a fault, ordering that the speechless woman:

...be taken back to the prison whence you came to a low dungeon, into which no light can enter; that you be laid on your back on the bare floor with a cloth around your loins but elsewhere naked; that there be set upon your body a weight of iron as great as you can bear and greater; that you have no sustenance except on the first day a morsel of coarse bread and on the second day three draughts of stagnant water from the pool nearest the prison door and on the third another morsel of coarse bread as before.

If after three days you are still alive, the weight will be taken from your body...

But this is where the 'judgement of penance' departed from its original purpose of extreme coercion and became a death trap from which there was no return; for the judge told the woman that if she was still alive after the three-day ordeal, she would have 'a large sharp stone placed beneath [her] back and the weight replaced'.

The penance of pressing continued for several decades after this, but this was the last time it was used explicitly as a death sentence. No surprise to learn that the victim's ghost is said to stalk the cells beneath the Shire Hall.

1688

GLORIOUS EFFUSIONS OF BLOOD

JAMES II, WHO reigned from 1685–9, was not as unpopular in Derby as elsewhere in the country. However, Robert Coke, Derby MP, head of the Derby militia and Deputy Lieutenant of Derbyshire, had other views on the subject. He, like many fellow MPs, had wanted the Catholic James legally excluded from the succession.

ABSOLUTE SO-AND-SO

James favoured Absolute Monarchy, a system without a written constitution in which the King's word is final, end of story. He also made plans to scrap the paranoid Test Act of 1673, which made all civil and military officials and courtiers swear an oath denouncing key aspects of the Roman Catholic Church.

Resistance was inevitable, and James slaughtered several rebel armies, notably the one led by his nephew, the pro-Republican Duke of Monmouth. He then increased the size of the standing armies in towns such as Derby, undermining the local militia and creating the kind of violent tensions associated with large groups of restless, underpaid men whose sole purpose in life is to fight.

James II, who increased Derby's standing army, causing chaos.

WILLIAM CAVENDISH: DERBYSHIRE'S REVOLUTIONARY SPELLING MISTAKE

* William Cavendish (1640–1707) was an experienced soldier and a staunch supporter of the Anglican status quo.

* He was one of the 'Immortal Seven' Englishmen who signed the letter inviting stadtholder of the Dutch Republic Willem van Orange-Nassau to take the English throne as William III.

* The 'Glorious Revolution' he helped to lead was also called the Bloodless Revolution. This title wasn't entirely accurate, though: there were two skirmishes in the south, much rioting in cities, and plenty of blood spilt in the wider arena of the Revolution in Ireland, Scotland and New England.

* In 1694 he was created Lord Steward, Marquess of Hartington and 1st Duke of Devonshire (having previously been the 4th *Earl* of Devonshire) for his services.

* The renowned womaniser financed the rebuild of Chatsworth House, Derbyshire, now the county's chief tourist magnet.

* It is said that the 'Devonshire' title was a seventeenth-century equivalent of a typo: it was supposed to be 'Derbyshire', a northern county that the southern scribe had never heard of.

Putting increasing pressure on public officers to formally consent to his religious, moral and social reforms, James now began to turf from office all opposition. Derby MP Coke defiantly declared in the House of Commons: 'I hope we are Englishmen, and not to be frightened with a few hard words!' His reward for this was a stint in the Tower of London.

When James produced an heir, the storm broke. Many, including Coke, believed that the child was not even the Queen's, but had been 'smuggled in inside a bedpan'. A deputation of MPs and aristocrats invited William, Prince of Orange, to invade and rule with his wife, James' Anglican sister Mary. William made landfall, and revolutionary William Cavendish, the Earl of Devonshire, arrived in Derby with 500 men to champion this latest revolution. At a dinner in his house on the Cornmarket, he spoke of 'calamities' threatening the country and the 'healing' that was necessary in order to prevent further disaster. The army, stationed here as a strong reminder of

King James' power, must have wondered which way the wind was going to blow.

The Duke told the men of Derby that he could 'think of no other expedient to compose our differences and prevent effusion of blood than... a Parliament freely and duly chosen'. He admitted that inviting over an army of invasion carried its own risks, but promised to fight to the death to defend the laws and religion of England, whatever happened.

Derby, as on many previous historical occasions, decided to embrace discretion over valour. There was, after all, a court-funded army in town...

BLOOD ORANGE

When troops arrived later that month bearing the Standard of the Prince of Orange, the Mayor refused to billet them in the town, striking a loyalist blow for King James. But pro-Revolution town officers sorted out lodgings for them instead.

William sailed across with his army – much smaller than James' – and some key English officers quit the army. The King panicked. His forces managed to cut down a small scouting party of William's in Somerset; but when James' daughter, Anne, abandoned his side, he had his own 'effusion of blood': a violent nosebleed, which he took as a bad omen. Swayed by the evidence on his handkerchief, he surrendered without further bloodshed, ending his reign by chucking the royal seal into the Thames (without which no lawful Parliament could be summoned) and, eventually, receiving safe passage to France.

William and Mary ascended the throne in February 1689, and Derby could have been forgiven for thinking it had seen the last of the Catholic Stuarts. The arrival in 1745 of James II's son, the Pretender Charles Edward, with his army of smelly rebels, soon put them right on that matter... but that's another story.

William III, ushered in by an 'effusion of blood'.

1718

POISON AT THE MILL!

JOHN LOMBE, SPY, adventurer and silk magnate, came to Derby in the early eighteenth century from Norfolk. His family ran a wool and silk business, and at an early age John had foreshadowed his future successes in the trade by refining the family's machinery and suggesting improvements. There were no experts in England to show the Lombes how to work the material properly, but John made it his ambition to fill the gap and equal the masters of the craft in Italy. He arrived in Derby with the intention of making his fortune in the industry.

At the end of the seventeenth century, a new silk mill named The Old Shop had been built in the town by businessman Thomas Cotchett (grandson of Mayor Thomas Sanders), and Lombe gained employment there. But the finer points of the weaving process were as yet beyond his skills, in spite of the Dutch machinery installed, which was at that time the best available. Lombe worked hard to improve the silk-throwing process – the twisting of silk filaments to form usable thread – but the mill's output remained relatively crude, and could not command the prices of the imported stuff from Italy.

NEW SILK IS A STEAL

Italy was the centre of excellence in the silk-weaving industry, and the factories in the Piedmont region and the island of Sardinia guarded their trade secrets with violent jealousy. With no prospect of expertise being shared, the only possible way of matching their output was to steal their technology.

Cotchett, opting for retirement, sold his concerns at the mill to John Lombe, who immediately appealed to his cousin, Thomas – who ran the family business back in Norfolk – to finance a trip to Italy. Thomas coughed up, and John took the tourist trail to the Continent in 1714, making his way to Piedmont and visiting the famous silk mills. The secrets of the process were not immediately obvious, and so Lombe took a crash course in Italian and used his silk tongue to get a job as a machine winder in one of the factories in Livorno.

Stealing the machinery designs was a dangerous endeavour, as Italy had harsh laws to deal with industrial spies, and anyone who pilfered technological ideas faced the death penalty. But Lombe was cool-headed, lingering after his shifts were over to make sketches, which were then smuggled back to England in silk bales prepared for export via agents hired by Thomas Lombe in Livorno.

QUICK ON THE DRAW

It was not long before John's after-hours activities aroused suspicion. Getting wind that Italian Government agents were on their way to question him, Lombe beat a hasty retreat, managing to board an English merchant vessel in the company of two Italian accomplices – but with the Piedmontese Navy soon hot on his tail, cannons blazing.

The English ship managed to outrun the guns, and John Lombe arrived back in Derby as the triumphant hero. His drawings were used to construct the necessary machinery, and a new five-storey silk mill was built in 1718 by Derby's foremost engineer, George Sorocold. The Lombes were awarded a patent from the Crown, and Derby silk of the finest quality could now undercut Italian imports and find its own worldwide markets.

The punchline to these adventures in espionage is that the revolutionary mill design drawings *had been in England all the time*! A sixteenth-century Italian book in Oxford's Bodleian Library contained full details of the silk-weaving method that Lombe had risked his life to acquire.

The Derby Silk Mill was the first factory in England, in the modern sense of the word – that is, a place in which the full processes of manufacture, and the full gamut of human misery, took place. It was

Industrial Museum and Silk Mill. (Photograph with kind permission of Andy Savage, www.derbyphotos. co.uk)

WHEEL OF MISFORTUNE

Beneath Derby Silk Mill's exciting exterior of espionage, murder and riches lies the real story of 1718: 300 mill employees, many of them children, slaving throughout the year for next to nothing.

Derby historian William Hutton recalled his own spell here between the ages of seven and fourteen as 'seven years' heart-ache'. He hated the work and everyone involved with it, rising at five each morning to be regularly beaten by his supervisor, and toiling alongside 'the most rude and vulgar of the human race, never taught by nature, nor ever wishing to be taught'.

Other visitors, escorted around the mill by its designer George Sorocold in the early days, commented on the thin, pasty-faced children, the beatings, the heat, the stink and the noise.

Writer and pamphleteer Daniel *Robinson Crusoe* Defoe, who visited Derby in 1724, describes how Sorocold nearly came a cropper during one of these tourist trips. He had assumed a position on some planks just above the mill wheel, and, in mid-eulogy, fell off. 'He was so very close to the sluice which let the water out upon the wheel... that tho' help was close at hand, there was no taking hold of him, till by the force of the water he was carried through, and pushed just under the large wheel, which was then going round at a great rate. The body being thus forc'd in between two of the plashers of the wheel, stopt the motion for a little while, till the water pushing hard to force its way, the plasher beyond him gave way and broke; upon which the wheel went again, and, like Jonah's whale, spewed him out... where he was taken up, and received no hurt at all'.

---

all driven by a single waterwheel of almost 7 metres in diameter, powering the most efficient engine of its day, and the building contained twenty-six winding engines, eight spinning mills and four twist mills, all laid out according to the appropriated Italian model.

So, thanks to Lombe's daring deeds, the silk industry boomed in England. The patented process was soon spinning a web of working-class industrial squalor in mills at Macclesfield, Chesterfield, Manchester, Stockport, London and, appropriately, Lombe's hometown of Norwich.

MURDER AT T'MILL

The Italians could not prevent England's silk industry from booming, but they could still take revenge on its progenitor. A counter-spy assassin was sent to Derby, a young Italian woman who, like a character in an espionage novel, gained a position at the silk mill in order to carry out her mission. The extravagantly wealthy John Lombe suspected nothing, probably assuming that Italians were all good at silk spinning and therefore natural candidates for employment. When he was found dead on 16 March 1722, the post-mortem showed that Lombe had been slowly poisoned over several months.

The woman was arrested, but acquitted through lack of evidence. She returned to her paymasters in Italy, and the fatal game of I Spy was over. Or was it? William Lombe, John's half-brother, inherited the Derby Mill, but in spite of the instant riches involved he fell into a depression, eventually taking his own life. The official verdict was simply 'a melancholy disposition', but of course the Hollywood version of the story could be very different...

Dreadful News from Derby!

With SANGUINEOUS photographs by ANDY SAVAGE

Lloyd's Evening Post (London), October 26, 1791 – THE BRUTAL BABY BODYSNATCHERS!

'Extract of a Letter from Derby: "One day last week, a lad was met coming into this town, having in his hand the skull of Matthew Cocklane, who was executed on the 21st of March 1776, for the murder of Mrs. Vickars, and afterwards hung in chains. It seems that the wind had blown him from his exalted situation the preceding night. His hair, skin, and most of his bones were in high preservation. Numbers, who had often stood in melancholy gaze, repaired to the gibbet, and returned with various parts of his remains."'

Morning Chronicle and London Advertiser, April 15, 1786:

'On Friday last, John Sheppard and William Stanley were executed at Derby... for house breaking. It appeared that Stanley had some thoughts of executing himself in prison, as on Wednesday morning when the cell was unlocked he refused to get up, and upon the keeper viewing him more particularly, he found that he had been trying how far he could effect his purpose by means of a large silk and cotton handkerchief, almost a new one, which he wore round his neck. He had made a proper noose, and only waited for an opportunity, by being left alone...

On Friday morning, when the executioner went to halter them, and tie their arms, he was observed by Sheppard to tremble; upon which he asked him the reason, saying nearly as follows, "Why do you tremble? we do not tremble."

After they were put into the cart several persons joined them; and as the procession moved on, Sheppard gave away oranges to some old acquaintance. Hymns were sung most of the way to the tree: a long time was there spent in prayer; this being over, Sheppard, in a kind of exstacy, took his fellow sufferer by the chin, and eagerly saluted him... Stanley desired [the crowd] would take warning, and concluded by saying, "Farewell, my boys, God bless you!"

After hanging the usual time, their bodies were cut down; Sheppard's friends took his to Dale Abbey for interment; Stanley was the same evening buried in St. Peter's church yard.'

Whitehall Evening Post (London), November 26, 1791

'Losses sustained by the overflowing of the Derwent on Sunday last: Thirteen lamb-ewes, the property of a Mr Radford, of Little Eaton, near Derby, were drowned, together with a ram which he hired for the season. Thirteen sheep were washed from a meadow near Breadsall, and twenty-five of them drowned; as was also a boatman (though an excellent swimmer) in re-crossing the Derwent at Borrowash, after having saved several sheep. It is said he was driven against the bridge by the strength of the current, and immediately sunk.'

Lloyd's Evening Post (London), July 4, 1792

'Saturday night, Jacob Cole, the beadle of All Saints' Church, Derby, drowned himself in the mill dam. He had met with two or three inter-ruptions in attempts on his life, but appeared fixed in his purpose; and it is said that, before he completed it, he sat himself down by the water-side, and smoked his pipe with the greatest of composure; which done, he walked deliberately into the water, and terminated a life too much addicted to intoxication. Previous to his going in, he wrote the following words on an adjoin-ing wall: "Jacob Cole lies in the mill-dam".'

Star (London), April 23, 1795:

'Friday se'nnight Thomas Nevill was executed at Derby... He was carried to execution in a mourning coach, attended by a hearse; where he assisted his executioner to fasten the rope to the tree, after which he drew his cap over his face, and leaped from the cart into eternity. Several persons witnessing this shocking scene had their pockets picked.'

Star, Saturday, March 16, 1799

'On Wednesday evening, Thomas Cocker, Fishmonger of Derby, was killed by the over-turning of his fish cart in that town, in returning from Burton Market.'

The Bury and Norwich Post: Or, Suffolk, Norfolk, Essex, Cambridge, and Ely Advertiser (Bury Saint Edmunds), October 23, 1816

'Mr Owen, of Derby, killed lately by the upset-ting of the mail, had not left his son's house five minutes, when he was returned a corpse. He put his head out of the coach window, when the spring broke, to see what was the matter, and the coach falling at the same moment, jammed his head between the carriage and the pavement.'

Examiner (London), January 17, 1841

'RAILWAY ACCIDENTS... Upon reaching a place called Chaddesdon, about a mile and a half from Derby, [an] engine became useless...

The night being very foggy, and no signal lamp apparent, the speed of [an incoming] train was kept at its usual pace (about twenty five miles and hour), and the engine came with much violence against the luggage train... the platform upon which the engine driver and stoker stand was doubled up, and both men received such injuries as to cause their deaths in about half an hour after the accident.

The "official" account of the disaster... states that "surgical attendance was at hand, and every care was taken of the parties". One of the passengers writes to say, "It was impossible, where we were, and at that hour, to obtain any surgical aid."'

The Bradford & Wakefield Observer; and Halifax, Huddersfield, and Keighley Reporter, February 11, 1847

HORRID MURDER AT DERBY – On Tuesday last, a man named James Cross, a gardener, residing in St. Peter's Street, Derby, murdered his wife, by cutting her throat... The daughter called in a neighbour named Mrs Osborne; but upon making her appearance Cross stabbed her in the neck and face, and would have murdered her had not the daughter seized and pinioned his arms. On searching Cross's house his wife was found with her throat cut. The poor crea-ture lay upon a bed in the chamber on the first floor up stairs. Her right hand was cut as if she had grasped the edge of the knife, and upon her wrist was a severe wound. One underneath her chin must have caused instant death... An inquest was held on the body on Thursday, and a verdict of wilful murder returned against Thomas Cross.'

The Derby Mercury, March 21, 1849

'Harold Strelly, aged 30, charged with having at the parish of St Werburgh, in the borough of Derby, wilfully murdered Samuel Tomlinson... George Bennett said – "On the 1st of December last I was keeper at Dr Brigstocke's Lunatic

Asylum, in Green-lane, Derby; on Thursday, the last day in November, I locked up prisoner and Samuel Tomlinson together... between six and seven the next morning I heard a noise of singing... I heard another noise, caused by one of the tin pots rolling on the floor; when I got in the room I saw Strelly standing near his bed, and Tomlinson lying on the floor; deceased was moaning then... I made Strelly get into bed, and went down stairs for a light. When I returned... Tomlinson was quite dead... when I examined the room I saw a lath [heavy piece of wood] standing near the bed."

...Prisoner here broke out, and addressing witness, said, "you have struck me many times". His Lordship ordered two persons to stand near the prisoner, and to prevent him from interrupting the Court.

Dr Brigstocke said – "I keep the Greenhill Lunatic private Asylum... I saw Tomlinson lying on his back, and a pool of blood near him; I examined the head of the deceased and observed a contused wound on the side of the head, and extending down to the mouth..."
Verdict, Not Guilty, on the ground of insanity.'

Market Place: one of the stall holders was crushed to death here. (Photograph with kind permission of Andy Savage, www.derbyphotos.co.uk)

All Saints': in 1792, the church usher drowned himself in the mill stream. (Photograph with kind permission of Andy Savage, www.derbyphotos. co.uk)

The Lady's Newspaper (London), March 23, 1850
'DERBY –TWO CHILDREN BURNT – A melancholy occurrence took place last week in Derby, by which two female children, daughters of a mill worker, were burnt to death. A little boy narrowly escaped the same fate. They had been locked in the house by the mother.'

John Bull (London), June 16, 1855
'DEATH OF TWO CHILDREN BY DROWNING – Two children of Mr Fairbanks, contractor, Derby, were drowned in the canal a few days ago. The little creatures – one six years old, the other three – were found clasped in each other's arms.'

The Bradford Observer, June 26, 1856

'MURDER NEAR DERBY – A murder was perpetrated on Monday evening last on the turnpike road... about two miles and a half from Derby. The murdered man is Enoch Stone, glove-hand, aged 47, residing in Spondon... The murdered man was robbed of his boots... Mr Stone was a harmless, inoffensive man, and has left a widow and five children to lament his sad fate.'

The Leeds Mercury, March 3, 1860

'At Derby, about four o'clock on Tuesday, when the storm seemed at its height, the point of the beautiful spire of St Alkmund's Church, including the vane and four feet of solid masonry, was blown down, and crashing through the church roof below, caused great injury, which will take a considerable sum of money to repair.'

John Bull (London), August 17, 1861

'Yesterday George Smith was executed at Derby, for the murder of his father at Ilkeston. There was a vast crowd of persons, and we regret to say the largest number were women.'

John Bull (London), August 24, 1861

'A remarkable service was held in St Michael's church, Derby, on Sunday last. George Smith, who was executed at Derby on the previous Friday, for the murder of his father, had made a confession, which was published, and which showed that he had led a most profligate life. The Vicar of St Michael's have notice... that at half-past eight o'clock he would address men only on the warnings to be drawn from this confession... A few minutes after the church doors were opened every seat was occupied, though all boys were turned back. There could not have been fewer than 500 men in the church, of all ranks and conditions, including very many who evidently were little accustomed to entering a church. Mr Clarke gave an earnest and plainspoken address on those special sins and temptations of impurity which cannot be pointedly dealt with in a mixed congregation... Such separate services would do something to check a species of sins which are fearfully common.'

THE FIRST AND LAST CRIMES OF RICHARD THORLEY:

FIRST: The Derby Mercury, April 21, 1852

'Richard Thorley, aged 16... pleaded guilty to stealing one cloth coat, the property of Charles Ward. Sentenced to four calendar months' imprisonment and hard labour.'

LAST: The Bury and Norwich Post, and Suffolk Herald, February 18, 1862

'On Friday night a man named Richard Thorley, employed at some iron works at Derby, murdered a young Irish girl called Murray [sic], whom he had courted, under the influence of jealousy. It appears that he proceeded to the house of the girl's mother, called her to the door, and deliberately cut her throat with a razor while he was caressing her'.

Nottinghamshire Guardian, February 18, 1862

'The inquest on the body of the hapless girl, Eliza Morrow, who was brutally murdered at Derby on Thursday, was held at the Town Hall, Derby, on Saturday. The surgical evidence showed that two wounds had been inflicted on the deceased's neck and throat, one of which had divided all the principal veins and arteries, and laid bare the lower jaw-bone, the right side of the base of the skull, and the upper vertebrae of the spine. Evidence was given showing that the prisoner Thorley had committed the injuries with the razor, which fell from the principal wound when the unfortunate deceased was found bleeding in the yard.'

Dundee Courier and Daily Argus, April 14, 1862

'Richard Thorley... was executed at Derby on Friday... A few evenings before the murder took place he saw her in the company of a soldier, and he then made up his mind to take away her life. He sharpened a razor, put it in his pocket, and called upon the woman at her own house... She followed him up the yard; they had words, and Thorley cut her throat with the razor.

St Peter's Street and churchyard: scene of murder, and the last resting place of criminals. (Photograph with kind permission of Andy Savage, www.derbyphotos.co.uk)

She screamed, and fell down, and, to use the murderer's own words, "he lay down by the side of her and drew the razor across her throat several times to stop her making a noise"... The wretched man rose between five and six o'clock on Friday morning... the procession then moved through the yard, headed by the chaplain, who read the burial service. The prisoners were drawn up in the different areas as the procession passed, and they called upon God to have mercy upon the wretched man's soul. At last the scaffold was reached, and as the chaplain commenced reading the service for the dead the bolt was withdrawn. A dense crowd, computed at 20,000, witnessed the execution.'

The Sheffield & Rotherham Independent, April 12, 1862

'Executioner Calcraft swiftly made the rope fast, shook the prisoner's hand, stepped from the drop, and Thorley was launched into eternity. He was fearfully convulsed, and at the first moment twisted round, his back being turned towards the crowd. Calcraft swiftly put his hand upon him and turned the face towards the mob, but he resumed the old position, and kept it till the body was cut down.'

The Derby Mercury, September 4, 1867

'DREADFUL STORM. Yesterday morning a fearful storm broke over Derby and the district. The lightning was nearly as vivid as a fortnight ago, and the thunder peals were sharp and loud. The rain poured down in heavy torrents, and it is anticipated that considerable damage has been done to the standing corn. We hear that several persons were injured in Derby, and we may expect to receive reports of damage done in various districts.

About twenty minutes to nine o'clock, on getting his breakfast, after milking, James White of Bleach-yard heard something coming down the chimney. The door of the cupboard was smashed, and all the crockery flew over the floor, and he said he felt a strange sensation on his right ear... He was very ill all day, and after the electric shock he went into a neighbour's house nearly double.

A man named William Allcock, in the same district, was also struck, and has sustained, it is feared, serious internal injuries.'

Leicester Chronicle and the Leicestershire Mercury, October 16, 1869

'FRIGHTFUL ACCIDENT ON THE MIDLAND RAILWAY. ...After the line had been cleared, a special train was prepared to convey those who had met with the most serious injuries at Derby Station. No time was lost in conveying the unfortunate excursionists to the Derby Hospital... Jane Parrot, 28 (married)... has received a severe compound fracture of the left leg, which has been amputated below the knee. Her right ear is also much torn, and her left side and arm badly contused, the process of amputation was most skilfully and successfully performed... the poor woman remains in a critical state.'

The Sheffield & Rotherham Independent, November 23, 1880

'About nine o'clock yesterday morning a young man named Alfred Saunders, was cut to pieces in a shocking manner on the Great Northern Railway at Little Chester, Derby. The deceased was employed by a cattle driver named Short to go to the goods yard to look after some cattle. For the purpose of shortening the distance, he commenced to walk from Little Chester along the line. When he arrived at the bridge which runs over the Derwent a goods train came up, but the deceased, being deaf, did not hear it approaching. He was knocked down, and his head and one of his arms were severed from his body.'

AND FINALLY:- DEATH at Derby:- An original survey of HORRIBLE true cases, collected TODAY by our SECRET REPORTER, Mr P.S.

1842: Forty-year-old Sarah Goddard was woken in the middle of the night by the sound of something falling in the coal-hole. Venturing downstairs, she saw three masked men staring back at her: they had lifted off the roof tiles to get in. She tried to escape, but they pummelled her about the face and head with a crowbar. They then ordered her to hand over all her money.

After taking what little she had, they left to search the rest of the house. About an hour later, when Sarah finally dared to leave her room, she discovered her sixty-nine-year-old sister, Martha, lying horribly wounded in the other bedroom. She was covered with blood from her head to her waist; pools of it covered the floor and bedclothes too. Martha had four holes in her skull, three of which had broken through the bone. There was a wound in her neck, and one of her fingers was broken. She had been struck with the same iron bar as her sister, and died a short while later. Her last words were, 'Sally, Sally – a man, a man!' It was the third time the sisters had been burgled, and it was thought that the same men had committed all the robberies.

The trial of her accused murderers at Derby – Samuel Bonsall and William Bland – and the pursuit of one further suspect, John Hulme, known as 'Jack the Sweep, alias Starbuck', had London papers buzzing as much as the Midlands titles that had first printed the story. Jack the Sweep was described as '27 and 30 years of age, and about 5ft 6ins or 7ins high; complexion and hair light; mouth rather on one side; nose a little turned-up; rather round-shouldered; and hangs his head down. Is a sweep, and usually dressed as such.'

Hundreds of Derby citizens tried to break down the court doors to get into the hearing. There the horrified listeners learned how Bonsall pulled out a knife and threatened to cut Sarah's throat; and how he 'knocked out [Martha's] brains with a crow-bar as she was getting out of bed'. On 5 April 1843, the papers

The Guildhall – the old Town Hall, venue for grisly murder inquests. (Photograph with kind permission of Andy Savage, www.derbyphotos.co.uk)

described the three men's executions. They silently processed from the condemned cells to the gallows at just after noon, where their arms were tied. They could be heard praying out loud, and begging for forgiveness, and one of them shouted 'Lord have mercy upon me! Christ have mercy upon me!' as the drop fell. Bonsall appeared to die almost instantly, and his two wicked accomplices perished at the end of their ropes shortly afterwards.

Trains delayed due to thieves on the line

1850: *The Times* reported on the 'Frightful Death of a Robber' on 3 October 1850. A thief had been spotted prowling about the station yard, but was not apprehended. When the 10 p.m. mail train pulled into the station, the engine-stoker sensed some kind of collision. The robber had avoided detection, but had not avoided the oncoming train. On examining the tracks his 'shockingly mangled' body was discovered, items of stolen train luggage scattered around him.

The Star Diver!

1868: The *Sheffield and Rotherham Independent* carried the story of 'Shocking Affair at Derby. Death of the Star Diver'. Twenty-two year old

Mr Worthington, self-styled 'Star Diver of the World', had been performing in the Derwent between Derby and Darley Grove on 7 May 1868. His show opened with some strange underwater feats, including drinking milk, peeling and eating an orange and playing the trumpet. He then threw a small boy into the torrent and successfully rescued him.

The finale involved a dive from a 35 metre high, purpose-built platform. Ascending and taking a few minutes to compose himself, the Star Diver jumped. 'In his progress downwards he made three evolutions of his body, and a medical gentleman on the bank remarked to some of the bystanders that he was a dead man. Worthington fell heavily on the top of the water on his side, and at once sank to the bottom of the river. The people seemed to expect that he would rise to the surface, as was his custom'. After a few minutes there was still no sign of him; and upon dredging up the body later it was decided that he had been concussed and died on impact.

Death is rubbish!

1870: As reported in the *Derby Mercury*, fire broke out in a three-storey house in Queen Street on 23 September 1870, and neighbours

Queen Street (from the cathedral), where burning rubbish roasted a man in 1870! (Photograph with kind permission of Andy Savage, www.derbyphotos.co.uk)

shouted for the occupant of the workshop on the top floor, a joiner called Robert Greatorex, to get out. When he failed to appear it was assumed that he had not been at home in the first place. When a witness confirmed this by mentioning that Greatorex had passed the spot a few minutes earlier, his signature pipe clutched between his teeth, there was great relief.

However, as the morbid mob kicked through the smoking rubble, 'a man pointed to what he thought a quantity of rubbish in one corner of the room. On examining this, however, Inspector Green was horrified to find that it was the charred remains of a human being... There was not a vestige of clothing about the body, the face and skull were one mass of burnt matter... the bowels were protruding, and no flesh was left.'

Almost-spontaneous combustion

1871: The Derby story reported in the *York Herald* on 4 February 1871 would be more at home in an *X-Files* script than a regional newspaper. The young Walker brothers were on their way to school in Babington Lane. Walking down Burghley Street, they noticed a black liquid substance on the road. One of them kicked at it, and it 'became one volume of fire'. In trying to put out the uncanny blaze, Abraham Walker accidentally touched it, immediately wiping his fingers on his shirt front.

The boys proceeded to school, but 'in a few seconds after Walker had been in the room his clothes took fire'. It took a long time to douse him, and he later died of severe burns. Rumour suggested that the mysterious substance was 'Greek Fire', a lethal cocktail of disputed chemical makeup invented by the ancient Byzantines and used in warfare up until the thirteenth-century: a type of Medieval napalm. Quite what it was doing on Burghley Street in 1871 is a different matter...

Death of a dedicated vendor!

1881: Thomas Orme sold the *Derby Mercury* in the Repton and Willington districts between Derby and Swadlincote, and had braved heavy snow to reach his loyal readers.

Travelling from Bridge Street in Derby at 5.30 a.m., he managed to sell all but two of his papers by the time he got to Newton Solney; but there the weather defeated him. He was discovered, frozen, in a ditch the following day. His rescuers took him to a nearby pub and tried to pour brandy down him, like human St Bernard dogs, but he died soon afterwards.

Mysterious Third-Class Assassination!

1898: The *Huddersfield Chronicle and West Yorkshire Advertiser* reported, 'On the arrival of the 9.35 express from London to Manchester at Derby, on Wednesday night, the dead body of a well-dressed middle-aged man was found in the third-class compartment. The deceased was shot through the head, and a revolver and 4 cartridges laid by his side. All papers and traces that could lead to his identity had been removed from his body, which now lies at Derby Infirmary.'

It was fifty years too early to blame the KGB, and the death remains a mystery.

1732

THE ART OF FLYING

IN 1732, ROBERT Cadman brought his high-wire 'steeple flying' act to the rooftops of England. In October the show came to Derby, with Cadman amazing the crowd by sliding down a rope suspended between the top of All Saints' (now Derby Cathedral) tower, one of the tallest in England, and the bottom of St Michael's, a steep descent at a distance of nearly 80 metres. He performed this feat on a wooden slide, with a groove to fit the rope, using just arms and legs for balance. Halfway across he blew a trumpet and fired a pistol, and he moved so fast that fire and smoke were observed in his wake.

Having descended, Cadman worked his way back up the rope again, entertaining the crowd on the way by dangling from various bits of his body. After the hour-long ascent he whizzed back down for a second time, performing this feat on three successive days. How did he manage to keep his nerve, his balance, and his life?

Well, he didn't. A few years later, in Shrewsbury, Cadman fell to his death. He is buried in that town, and his grave epitaph describes, poetically, exactly what happened:

Let this small monument record the name
Of Cadman, and to future times proclaim

How, by an attempt to fly from this high spire,
Across the Sabrine stream, he did acquire
His fatal end. 'Twas not for want of skill,
Or courage to perform the task, he fell;
No, no, a faulty cord being drawn too tight
Hurried his soul on high to take her flight,
Which bid the body here beneath, good-night.

Hogarth's painting 'Cadman the Steeple-Flyer' commemorates this genuine celebrity.

FLYING DONKEY FLATTENS CROWD

The vogue in Derby for *al fresco* 'flying' escapades was short-lived but exciting. During the brief craze, lots of people scaled the heights, attaching ropes to everything from walls and houses to trees and poles, and either contriving their own means of descent, or sending unfortunate cats and dogs up and down instead.

The craze came to an end in August 1734, when a vagrant man appeared in town and boasted that he would better Cadman's performance (the bit before he died, that is) of two years before.

FREAKSHOWS, BLOOD SPORTS AND OTHER PUB GAMES

Crowd-pulling acts such as the rope-men were usually funded by public houses, on the safe assumption that the landlords would reap the benefit of boosted drinks sales.

The high-wire craze was fleeting, but safer acts were a constant feature of the Derby scene, from freak shows of dwarfs, giants and misshapen humans, to intelligent dogs, animal shows and stuffed mermaids. The Wheatsheaf in the Market Place appears to have been the busiest patron of this type of entertainment.

Cock-fighting was another great crowd pleaser, and a new cockpit was constructed at Nun's Green, Friargate, in 1617, to match the one at Cockpit Hill. This hugely popular sport appealed to upper and lower classes alike (and was eventually abolished by the disapproving middle classes in the nineteenth century), involving as it did a winning combination of blood and betting.

At the even less reputable end of the blood-sports scale, some Derbeians staged fights and baitings between various mammals, including dogs, badgers and hedgehogs. Bear-baiting was a rare treat, and bull-baiting sometimes beefed up the action. In these bouts, the animal was tied to a stake by a rope attached to the ring through its nose, and savage dogs, specially trained, were released to attack it. Sometimes fireworks were hung over the bull, or attached to hooked barbs which were stabbed into its skin. 'There's such a confus'd Noise,' said one description of 1709, 'of Rockets, Serpents, Squibs, Crackers, and ink-Horn Guns that you can scarce distinguish one from another. Take care below, Gentlemen! See how the Bull raves and tears, kicks, flings and bounces, that if ye be not aware he'll be among ye!' Sometimes the bull would indeed manage to break free, and charge the crowd.

Such sports were banned by the Cruelty to Animals Act of 1835.

He attached one end of his rope to All Saints', as his predecessor had done, but fixed the other to the County Hall in St Mary's Gate, a distance more than twice the length of the Cadman descent. Having secured his tightrope, he then led a donkey into the church and coaxed it up the stairs of the tower. According to Victorian historian Stephen Glover, by the time of the performance it 'had been braying several days at the top of the steeple for food; but, like many a lofty courtier for a place, brayed in vain'.

When the appointed hour came, the man amazed everyone by descending the rope at speed, towing a wheelbarrow with a thirteen-year-old boy in it. Then it was the turn of the poor donkey. It had been fastened to a wooden board similar to the one used by Cadman, with lead weights attached to each of its legs to secure it in a position worthy of the best torturer.

With the rope being slack, and the weight of the animal and its leaden burden being considerable, onlookers had the impression that, for the first part of the descent, the animal was simply plummeting. The braying beast then whizzed down the final hair-raising stretch towards County Hall. Twenty metres short, the rope snapped. By this point the animal was moving at a terrific speed, and it flattened several rows of onlookers.

According to Glover: '...he bore down all before him. A whole multitude was overwhelmed; nothing was heard but dreadful cries; nor seen, but confusion. Legs and arms went to destruction. In this dire calamity, the ass, which maimed others, was unhurt itself, having a pavement of soft bodies to roll over.'

The plummeting rope at the All Saints' end knocked down chimneys and injured more people. But although there were broken bones and blood aplenty, there were no reported fatalities. The heir of Cadman counted his blessings, but was unable to count his intended whip-round money, as a hasty exit was in order. The fate of the ass is not recorded. Its former owner hid himself and left Derby before anyone could arrest him. 'This dreadful catastrophe put a period to the art of flying', says Glover.

NO ROPE, NO NET

The excitement at the top of All Saints' tower was not over yet, though. In 1735, a man climbed the steeple in order to fix some holes in the lead on the roof.

dHe made a fire on a hearth of loose bricks (probably needing constant access to a kettle, like all good workmen), and left it to burn itself out afterwards. A few days later smoke was seen billowing from the battlements, and it took a long time for anyone to pluck up the courage to climb the tower and sort it out. They arrived just in time: the lead was melted, and many of the supporting beams had burnt away too. The fire was doused, and disaster averted.

The last 'steeple flyer' was probably the poor dog that historian William Hutton saw fall from the top of the high tower of All Saints', some time in the mid-eighteenth century. He was 'surprised at the length of time he took in his descent, owing to his beating the air in his struggles to rise'.

1732

SEX AND DEATH: THE BEARE NECESSITIES

BY **1732, JOHN** Hewit, a thirty-year-old butcher from Stepping Lane in Derby, had lost interest in his wife Joan. Receiving nothing from him but violence and contempt, Joan Hewit turned to the bottle.

Eleanor Beare, who ran the Crown Inn, offered Hewit the solace of her bedroom and used her considerable charm and beauty to win his affections, full as she was with contempt for her own husband, Ebeneezer. Joan Hewit, meanwhile, spent an equally large amount of time in the Crown Inn glugging the liquid refreshments and complaining, quite justly, of her hard lot. But Eleanor Beare's ears were not the most sympathetic, especially where the subject of the griping was her lover. It soon came into her head to murder the poor old drunkard.

Beare was no stranger to death, as another of her sidelines involved taking unwanted newborns from their mothers and disposing of them. This was murder in the eyes of the law, although inducing abortions, which was another of her sources of income, was not a statutory crime at the time, even when carried out with the crude implements that Beare favoured.

The love triangle was squared by Rosamund Ollorrenshaw. She worked at the pub, and had soon won a place in John Hewit's heart that threatened to oust the dangerously jealous Eleanor. But first things first, and the initial obstacle was drunken Joan Hewit.

DEATH BY PANCAKE!

Beare, with pretence of friendship, invited Joan over to eat pancakes at the Crown, personally mixing the batter of flour, milk, eggs, a pinch of salt and a larger pinch of arsenic. Rosamund Ollorrenshaw, who probably had no suspicion of the drastic addition to the recipe, was the cook. Mrs Hewit tucked in, and three hours later she was dead.

An autopsy identified the cause of death easily enough: this had doubtless been Beare's plan all along, to implicate the unwitting chef. She was said to have poisoned 'unwanted' wives before, for money. All three – Eleanor, John Hewit and young Rosamund – were arrested. At the trial, John soon saw that he had no way out, but perhaps he could still save one of his lovers. When Rosamund was asked if her mistress knew the pancakes were poisoned, Hewit stepped on her toe. It was an ambiguous prompt, but probably meant 'say that she did, and save your life!'

Sadly, Rosamund took it the opposite way, answering 'No'. This implied to the judge that the younger woman was the sole poisoner, acting willingly on Hewit's command.

By the day of execution Rosamund could barely walk, and it is said that she expired in the gallows cart before the rope could do its work. John Hewit was observed to have behaved with great tenderness and devoutness on the day, which inspired great pity from the onlookers, while Rosamund was mourned afterwards as a tragic loss.

Morledge, where Eleanor ran for her life. (Photograph with kind permission of Andy Savage, www.derbyphotos.co.uk)

ORDEAL BY ORDURE

None of this did much good for trade at the Crown Inn, nor for the relative light in which Eleanor Beare was viewed. Public opinion maintained that, although acquitted at the trial, she was the only truly guilty one. Efforts were made at the next Derby Assizes to make her pay for the loss of three lives, by bringing into the spotlight her operations as abortionist and attempted poisoner.

Historian William Hutton wrote in 1791: 'though these were crimes of an atrocious nature, and sufficiently blackened by the counsel, yet, being unknown to the law, except by the vague name of *misdemeanors*, it had not provided an adequate punishment.' The harshest sentence that could be passed in the circumstances was two one-hour sessions in the town pillory on consecutive Fridays (market day), and three years in gaol.

Hutton remembered the pillory episode well: 'I saw her, August 18, 1732, with an easy air ascend the hated machine, which overlooked an enraged multitude. All the apples, eggs, and turnips, that could be bought, begged, or stolen, were directed at her devoted head. The stagnant kennels were robbed of their contents, and became the

cleanest part of the street. The pillory, being out of repair, was unable to hold a woman in her prime, whose powers were augmented by necessity: she released herself; and, jumping among the crowd, with the resolution and agility of an Amazon, ran down the Morledge, being pelted all the way; new kennels produced new ammunition; and she appeared a moving heap of filth. With difficulty they remounted her; and I saw the exasperated brother of the unfortunate Rosamund pull her with violence into the pillory by the hair. A human being in distress excites commiseration, whatever is the cause. Her punishment exceeded death. By the time they had fixed her, the hour had expired, and she was carried to prison, an object which none cared to touch.'

RISE OF THE HIGHWAYWOMAN

On the next Friday, Eleanor Beare seemed not just bruised, but bent and swollen out of shape. The pillory keeper, however, seeing though the ruse, removed her head gear, which turned out to consist of twelve layers of cloth and a piece of pewter, to protect her from the potentially lethal missiles that would be headed her way. The 'severe peltings of the mob' reduced her to a bloody mess, which was afterwards shovelled into the gaol, a stone's throw from the Crown Inn.

Three years later she re-emerged from prison, but within a few months she was back inside. Free a second time, in 1740 she turned to highway robbery, hijacking a wagon convoy on the Ashbourne Road and provoking a riot, for which crime she was transported for seven years.

Historian Hutton prefers a happier ending, though, stating that after the first imprisonment: 'She... recovered her health, her spirits, and her beauty; and at her enlargement [i.e. release] was preceded by a band of music. She died in the meridian of life.'

TRANSPORTS: THE ORIGINAL EX-PATS

* Transportation was a punishment for serious crimes, and a very handy one for Governors of penal colonies, whose inmates were used for slave labour.
* Eleanor Beare would have been sent to either Virginia or the West Indies. The chances of her returning after the seven-year sentence were slim: an English folk song of transportation to Virginia puts the odds this way: *Oh England, sweet England, will I never see you more? If I do it's ten thousand to twenty!*
* The first records of Derby transports are from 1732, although people were probably being sent before then.
* Later in the eighteenth century, Australia became the main destination, with the American Revolution putting an end to the transatlantic transport traffic.
* Several families in Australia have traced their roots back to Derby felons, such as the Beauchamps of New South Wales, who are descended from Stephen Wain, transported for theft in 1800.

1745

THE INVASION OF DERBY

ON 3 DECEMBER 1745, the Duke of Devonshire gathered his levied army of 750 'Derbyshire Blues' at the George Inn in Derby. The men were paid, armed and ready to march north-west to join other Royalist forces in fighting off the invasion of Charles Edward Stuart – Bonnie Prince Charlie – son of James II and Pretender to the English throne.

The Prince and the Jacobite rebels were relying on the still-simmering loyalty of the English, who were believed to have no love for the pudding-headed Hanoverian George I who had succeeded Queen Anne, the last of the Stuart monarchs. Charlie also needed the support, and physical presence, of the French army, which had promised to help mop up any armed English resistance. And by the time he made it down from Scotland to Preston in Lancashire, things were going reasonably well – although the French had yet to put in an appearance.

The Duke of Devonshire told his modest militia that the Duke of Cumberland was about to engage the Jacobites in the north-west, and that they were to join him shortly. However, an hour later the flustered Duke broke the news that this wasn't the case at all, and that the vanguard of the rebel army was actually in Ashbourne, just up the road from Derby.

HOPES SCOTCHED

Confusion reigned. The Duke marched his Blues away to Nottingham that evening, not wishing to face Charlie's 9,000 men with his 750. Many businesses boarded up their premises and fled town too. On the morning of 5 December, bells were rung and bonfires lit to welcome the vanguard of the Jacobite force, probably a peace offering more than genuine celebration.

The rebels, mounted on horseback, were looking in pretty good shape considering their long trek, and, descending on the George Inn – recently vacated by the Duke of Devonshire – they informed the Derby magistrates that they would need lodging and food for 9,000 men (in reality the number was probably closer to 7,500). A few hours later the main host arrived, marching to bagpipes, and in stark contrast to the posh ones on horseback. According to a first-hand account in the *Derby Mercury*:

...a parcel of shabby, lousy, pittiful [sic] looking fellows, mixed up with old men and boys, dressed in dirty plaids, and dirty shirts without breeches, and wore their stockings made of plaid, not much above half way up their legs, and some without shoes or next to none, and numbers of them so fatigued with their

71

Queen Anne, the last Stuart monarch.

long march, that they really commanded our pity more than our fear.

The Scots requested that Prince Charlie's arrival be proclaimed in the Market Place, and at dusk he finally appeared on foot, making straight for Exeter House, the most upmarket lodgings in town.

Semi-apocryphal stories abound. It is said that an attempt by Derby's Mayor Robert Hague to seek audience with Charlie at Exeter House was greeted by a kick from one of the guards that sent him back down the stairs with the words: 'Rascal that ye are, if ye want tae see a Pretender, get ye tae St James!' (i.e. to George I in London). This is possibly why Hague wrote a grovelling letter to George I in the aftermath, telling of 'the inexpressible horrors and confusion they brought hither, attended in many instances with violent and open acts of rapine and plunder'.

HOUSEGUESTS FROM HELL

One of the residents whose house was billeted by the Jacobite army described the experience afterwards. Complaining of their shoddy attire, he revealed what the Scots really wore under their kilts: '…under their plaids nothing but a various sort of butchering weapons were to be seen: the sight at first must be thought shocking and terrible.'

But his chief concern was hygiene: 'My hall (after these vagabond creatures began to be warm, by such numbers under the straw, and a great fire near them) stunk so of their itch, and other nastinesses about them, as if they had been so many persons in a condemn'd hole, and 'twill be very happy if they have left no contagion behind them. I cannot omit taking notice of the generous present they made me at parting on Friday morning, for the trouble and expense I was at, and the dangers undergone… which was a regiment of lice, several loads of their filthy excrements, and other ejections of different colours…'

A GAME OF HIDE AND STREAK

Eliezer Birch was a key player in the Jacobite downfall, thanks to his misinformation under interrogation.

After being grilled by the Prince's intelligence officers, Birch was locked in one of the bedrooms at Exeter House. But on the morning of 6 December, he noticed that his guards were distracted by Prince Charlie's frantic preparations for departure.

Seizing the opportunity, Birch forced open a window and jumped. Stunned by the 6-metre plummet, he staggered round the wall into the garden next door, losing his footing where the wall met the riverbank and plunging into the Derwent.

Turning adversity into advantage, Eliezer clambered out and left his clothes, watch and small change in a riverside building; he then jumped back in, swam naked down the weir, and then downstream for three miles to Alvaston (where a farmer's wife gave him clothes, shelter, and five out of ten due to the effects of icy water).

Evading pursuers, Birch managed to get to Nottingham on horseback, only to discover that the Jacobites had retreated. On the following day he was back in Derby, but his clothes and valuables had 'done a Jacobite' and disappeared.

It was also reported in the ever-indignant middle-class press that Jacobite soldiers stole at will, using threats, cocked pistols and drawn swords, 'so that several persons were obliged to abscond to preserve their lives'; whereas more reliable reports suggest that that they were, on the whole, well behaved. The Duke of Devonshire's son wrote in a letter that he 'was surpris'd to find they had done so little damage', and they were remembered for their civility and lack of personal hygiene rather than high-handedness or aggression. Indeed, many townsfolk seem to have genuinely welcomed the invaders, one old lady even distributing white cockades for everyone to wear.

TAXING TIMES

The Jacobites' one truly unpopular dictate was that all outstanding taxes and excise monies should be stumped up for the cause, and that everyone named on a list as subscribers to the Duke of Devonshire's regiment should pay an equal amount to Prince Charlie's. Other extortions were made, and all horses confiscated; but the atmosphere remained calm, perhaps even supportive. It is almost certain that later stories about cannons being levelled at the Guildhall to reinforce a demand for money are untrue.

But Derby, as so often in its history, seems to have veered towards the status quo rather than the revolutionary. The Scots' efforts to recruit Derbeians resulted in just six conscripts, according to the *Derby Mercury*. At most the figure seems to have been forty: hardly the upsurge the Prince would have hoped for.

Charlie's plans for what to do next were heavily influenced by bogus intelligence supplied by Georgian spies, one of whom, Eliezer Birch, was captured and brought to Exeter House for interrogation. Birch revealed under torture that the road to London was blocked by the English army. Even though a Jacobite vanguard had secured safe passage south over Swarkestone Bridge, and succeeded in making it all the way to Loughborough and back (to be fêted as returning heroes), the misinformation was taken on board.

Other spies played down the support that the rebels could expect further south; and certainly the lack of conscripts in Derby must have influenced the catastrophic decision to turn north once again and return to Preston. In reality there was no army blocking the south road, and the way to London (and the planting of a firm Jacobite boot up a flabby Hanoverian bottom) was clear.

The devious intelligence left the invaders in disarray, and they left on the morning of 6 December:

> ...all in a great hurry: many of their men left their horses, swords, pistols, targets, shot, powder, bullets and other odd things behind them where they quartered: a plain proof of their confusion. Their pretended Prince, mounted upon a black horse... left his lodgings about 9 o'clock, and riding cross the market-place went through the Rotton Row, then turned down Sadler-gate towards Ashbourn [sic], preceded and followed by the main body of his army. We were rid of them all (except a few stragglers) by 11 o'clock.

OVERRULED AND OVERPOWERED

The French reinforcements never arrived; the flocking to the cause of a Stuart Restoration didn't materialise; and a combination of clever spies and bad decisions destroyed the Rebellion. In spite of Charlie actually favouring an attack, he bowed to the decision of his generals not to confront the army of the Duke of Cumberland, which was then encamped in Coventry. The rebels trekked back to combine with the rest of their forces in Scotland, and for their fatal tryst with Armageddon at the Battle of Culloden near Inverness on 16 April 1746.

The Jacobite army's retreat from Derby is one of history's great missed opportunities. As historian Robert Simpson wrote in 1826:

> ...had the conduct of the individuals which composed it, been as ferocious and brutal as that which disgraced the victorious party after the battle of Culloden, their footsteps would have been marked with blood; and the names of thousands, who are now living happy in the bosom of their families, become extinct for ever.

1817

REFORM RIOTS, PART 1

THE THREE MEN who prepared to defend themselves on charges of High Treason – the gravest offence in the land – in the Shire Hall at Derby in 1817 were examples of the frustrated multitude of Georgian citizens who had simply had enough. Their starting point had been stark and simple: the poor were overworked, overtaxed, overlooked and, in this pre-suffrage, pre-Union era, not represented at any level of society. Parliamentary reform of a radical nature was needed, otherwise England would have to follow the path of France into bloody revolution. The English radical Tom Paine had already shown the way, and it was just a case of getting on with it.

But successive administrations had seemed either indifferent or impotent when faced with the plight of the underclass. Petitions were ineffectual, a byword for waste paper; and the Government seemed to have spies and constables everywhere, taking names and putting pressure on potential troublemakers. Well-meaning, honest MPs (a rare enough breed) never seemed to win the argument in the House of Commons, and all the breath spent on pushing reform went to waste. Hence, those three men facing charges of High Treason in 1817...

BLOODY SOLDIERS AND OTHER VERMIN

This head-against-a-brick-wall situation eventually tipped a revolutionary named Jeremiah Brandreth over the edge. Knowing that his words would be reported to the last syllable, he chaired a meeting of poor labourers for four hours in a pub at Pentrich, some 12 miles north of Derby, saying, in brief, that it was time to overturn the Powers That Be. To make the event as newsworthy as possible, he is alleged to have spoken partly in verse:

> Every man his skill must try,
> He must turn out and not deny;
> No bloody soldiers must we dread:
> We must turn out and fight for bread.
> The time is come, you plain must see,
> The Government opposed must be!

He added that 'every village should kill its own vermin!'

Brandreth set out his plans to seize arms, attack or set fire to strategic buildings, shoot a few people, and enlist popular support from the working-class slaves of Derbyshire, Sheffield and beyond. Bullets were to be manufactured from church roof lead, gunpowder was to be purloined, and the towns and cities of the nation would surely rise up in arms. London itself would soon be stormed, the old order would be ousted, and the Revolution would install representatives whose foremost concern was the wellbeing of the poor. All this was to begin in nearby South Wingfield tomorrow evening.

Tomorrow evening came, but less than thirty supporters turned out, swelling to a couple of hundred by the time events had reached their climax. Undeterred, Brandreth and his right-hand man William Turner led the revolutionaries out for their tryst with history, armed with guns, swords and pikes. Their first victim was a farm servant, shot when he refused to cooperate – which was hardly the resounding blow against the landowners that Brandreth had been looking for. Back in Pentrich, a few torched houses and several extortions later, it was clear to many that popular support was simply not forthcoming.

Brandreth's plan was to join fellow revolutionaries in Nottingham, but before they got there they were scattered by the Derbyshire Yeomanry and the 15th Hussars. By now, the surrounding countryside was on maximum alert. The Derby Mayor mobilised five units of soldiers to defend the town, but the feared attack never came. The revolutionaries were hauled in one by one, with Brandreth captured on 22 July. They were all slung into gaol, many in Derby, to await a special Assize that had been fixed for 15 October.

HANGING, DRAWING AND QUARTERING, WITHOUT THE MESSY BITS

Ironically, given the motives behind the uprising, many of the prisoners got off lightly because they were so obviously poor and without influence: clearly dupes of cleverer men such as Brandreth, declared the Justices. An impressive 300 jurymen and 208 witnesses were summoned to the show trial, and it took several days to go through the motions. On the 18th, sentence was passed on Jeremiah Brandreth; and between then and the

---

TAKING A DROP

The block upon which the four Pentrich Revolutionaries' heads had been lopped was kept for macabre posterity, and can be seen in the Derby Museum.

The 1817 Revolutionaries were hanged at the 'New Drop' near Derby Gaol. This featured a drop-platform through which prisoners could descend for maximum ease of dispatch.

The New Drop replaced the old-fashioned open gallows at Gallows Baulk, at which victims had stood on wagons, which were then driven away to produce the desired effect.

Other colourful victims of the Drop included:

* Sixteen-year-old Hannah Bocking, on 22 March 1819, for killing her companion with a poisoned cake on the way to herd cattle in a field near Derbyshire's last gibbet at Wardlow Mires.
* Thomas Hopkinson, on 2 April 1819, for highway robbery. He had been one of Brandreth's arsonists in 1817, getting off the hook by informing against his comrades.
* Forty-year-old George Batty, 8 April 1825, for 'ravishing' a sixteen-year-old.
* In April 1833, John Leadham had the dubious honour of being the first person executed at the new county prison, which had opened in 1828, for the capital crime of bestiality.

25th, William Turner and Isaac Ludlam – deemed the other chief perpetrators – joined him on Derby's death row.

The three were sentenced to be executed in public by hanging, drawing and quartering, the good old-fashioned punishment for High Treason. The goriest bits were to be omitted, however, the nineteenth-century being more squeamish than its predecessors.

The Best Last Words award went to the brave Ludlam, who said as part of his prayer:

'Bless the King of this nation, bless all the people, high and low, rich and poor, bond and free; yea, bless all, from the King upon his throne down to the meanest subject in the realm, and may this awful dispensation be made a blessing to thousands and tens of thousands!'

They were hanged outside the gaol, and their lopped heads were held up for the crowd to behold, as a warning to any other poor labourer who might be feeling a bit revolutionary.

1831

REFORM RIOTS, PART 2: BLOOD IN THE STREETS

IN 1831, **PARLIAMENT** prepared to vote on the Reform Bill, brought in by the Whig Party. If it became an Act it would enable more people to vote in elections, finally removing the iron grip of the ruling landowners, who had not welcomed any form of suffrage or power sharing since their ancestors had first seized the reins of the state in 1066. After heated debate, it passed through the House of Commons successfully, and was put before the Lords on 8 October 1831. The votes came in: for, 158; against, 199. News of this defeat arrived in Derby at 7 p.m. – and the rioters were ready.

DEATH TO THE TORIES!

Funeral peals rang all day from All Saints' and St Peter's, fires lit the sky, and gangs of enraged men stormed the streets. During this first outing the riots consisted largely of tradesmen and craftsmen who would have benefited from the reform, rather than the landless workers who would have remained voteless anyway.

The windows of Derby's leading Tories, the enemies of the Bill, were stoned mercilessly. There was no police force in the town as such, and no one was daft enough to confront the men.

Some Tories, such as Alderman Thomas Eaton, donned disguises and fled town. A known champion of reform, banker William Baker appeared before his property at 44 Friar Gate and entreated the crowd to disperse, arguing that it would damage his (and their) great cause. He was cheered and treated to a few gentle projectiles. Bricks were then put through any glass that had been overlooked in the houses of the chief Tory victims, while Sir Robert Wilmot's windows, gardens and other exteriors at Chaddesden Hall were trashed with great thoroughness.

JAIL BREAK, DEATH AND DESTRUCTION

After a late night, the rioters retired to consider their next move, and were not impressed on the following morning when two of their number were reported to have been gaoled. They broke up a public meeting called by Mayor Charles Lowe to discuss and thereby defuse the situation, and marched to the recently converted gaol annex in Friar Gate. They beat on the doors with an uprooted cast-iron lamp stand and secured release for their two companions, along with the other twenty-one prisoners enjoying the facilities at the time.

The angry protesters now moved to the main gaol, a new edifice on Vernon Street; but this time they met with resistance. The guards had guns, and four men were shot – one of them, John Garner, falling dead on the spot. This shook the rioters considerably, and they listened afterwards to the pleas of four respected Reformist magistrates.

The men dispersed; however, by the afternoon another riotous assembly had regrouped, now determined to take advantage of the situation by looting and mugging. The all-out rampage sent most other Derbeians back behind locked and bolted doors. There were at least two murders in the streets, which provided sufficient excuse for bringing in the army. The Riot Act was read, and the soldiers of the Nottingham 15th Hussars piled in. Several men were injured in the pitched battle with stones and bullets, the Hussars using their sabres and carbines to win the day.

In the aftermath, Special Constables were sworn in to police the town; but, after a few minor skirmishes, by 12 October it was all over.

ONE WAY TICKETS TO AUSTRALIA

Ringleaders were not tried until the Derby Spring Assizes of 1832. Eleven men appeared before the judge, who, in the interests of peace, acquitted all but two of the most conspicuous looters and muggers, who were transported to Australia. The new town gaol was reinforced, and towers were added to each end.

Elsewhere in the country, further riots flared up, making the Establishment consider the possibilities of civil war. The brink of Revolution receded later in 1832, when the Duke of Wellington, Arthur Wellesley's Tory Government was defeated, and Lord Grey's Whigs assumed power. The Reform Bill was resurrected speedily, and this time it got through both Houses and became law. This was followed in 1835 by the Municipal Corporations Act, which brought democracy to local politics.

So all was happy and harmonious from hereon in? Far from it...

DERBY MERCURY OCTOBER 1831: QUOTES FROM THE INQUEST

'The Coroner briefly addressed the jurors, observing they were assembled to enquire into the manner in which several persons had come by their deaths...

John Garner, aged 17 years ... received a gun shot wound in the abdomen on the 9th instant, in front of the county gaol ... 14 or 15,000 persons ... commenced swearing and throwing Stones; many were drunk, disorderly, riotous ... The governor warned them of his intention to fire ... witness saw a young man fall, and heard the mob cry out he was shot ... the deceased said, knowing that he was dying, that he ... heard the men declare they would pull down the stones of the gaol ... and expecting a disturbance he was turning to go away when he received the shot ... Two other witnesses [said] there were no disturbances, no threats, no stones thrown at the entrance of the gaol... A verdict of justifiable homicide.

Inquest on the death of John Hickin: a soldier came riding up. "A shot was fired, the ball passed through my hat, and struck a man who was on the pavement ... I did not at first know what had happened to my hat; I turned to look, and saw the man down; I heard him groan, and saw him bleeding." [The hat with the hole was produced in evidence]. The man felt very much affected on seeing the gun levelled, and persons opposite, as he thought some one must fall a victim; he saw the soldier fire, and the deceased fall, and wished to go to his assistance but was afraid of being shot; the soldier sat and reloaded his piece, and then turned away ... A verdict of accidental death.'

1834

STRIKE!

IN NOVEMBER 1833, Peet and Frost, silk-hose manufacturers of Bridge Street, Derby, sacked a man for producing substandard work. In a stand of solidarity, 800 men at the factory refused to work until the sacked man had been reinstated. By February the following year, over 2,000 silk workers were on strike. On 11 February they marched in peaceful protest through Derby, and on the 12th they congregated in Spondon, stopping the annual street football game.

SACK 'EM ALL!

Peet and Frost were unmoved by all this, drafting in workers from outside Derby, mainly London, to continue the work. Their factory was among the twenty businesses whose names were attached to a declaration ('The Declaration of Twenty') reproduced in the *Derby Mercury* on 4 December 1833 complaining about the 'Trade Union' that had formed. 'The members of the Union,' it claimed, 'are bound by a secret oath, and their admission is accompanied by mystical ceremonies, calculated and designed to impose upon and overawe the minds of credulous and unsuspecting men, and render them the unconscious slaves, and ready tools, of their more crafty

leaders.' The resolve of the undersigned was: 'THAT each of them will immediately cease to employ every man who is a Member of the Trades' Union, and will not receive or take back into service any man who continues to be a Member.'

BLACK SHEEP CULLING

The men brought in from outside Derby were dismayed to find that they were universally hated. In January 1834, these maligned and aggrieved men published a communal statement in the *Derby Mercury*. Part of their passionate plea asked 'whether we are not fulfilling the duties we owe to our families, and to Society better, by seeking honest employment here, than by continuing in London in idleness, poverty and misery?'

Certainly not, according to a statement published a few days earlier by *Pioneer*, the Trades Union Magazine:

Ba! Ba! Ba! – More Black Sheep – Nine more willing slaves have left London for Derby. Let us put them on our black list in our *Pioneer*... The finger of scorn will be pointed at them whithersoever they go. They will be miserable outcasts in society. We would advise them to assemble under

THE WORKHOUSE: KICKING UP A STINK

Workhouses were for old or infirm paupers, and the unemployed. Conditions were grim, and this was partly to deter what the modern tabloid press would term 'scroungers'. Work was provided to those who were able, but was paid only in meagre food, clothing and shelter. These work opportunities had to be taken, regardless of your fitness for the task, otherwise you might forfeit your right to remain in the workhouse.

Inmates were not allowed to play truant. The *Derby Mercury* reported on 19 August 1840: 'Philip Spencer was brought up, charged with having been an inmate of the Derby Union workhouse, and absconding therefrom without leave, taking with him the clothes provided him by such Union. Committed to the house of correction for one calendar month.' (The house of correction was a kind of prison-cum-workhouse for beggars and vagrants.)

The workhouse was a grim place for anyone with a sense of smell. In May 1840, the Governor of Derby Workhouse complained of 'the want of a proper ventilated place to lay out the Dead. Hitherto we have occupied... Refractory Wards for that purpose, but for want of proper Ventilation have found them very obnoxious on account of the putrid effluvia being so confined.' In the same month the Governor noted: 'the water closets... are very much out of order somewhere, and the stench is becoming very unpleasant.' To add to the general nastiness, individual chamber pots had, due to breakages, recently been replaced by communal buckets.

the wall of their present confinement, and there... pair off, in couples of equal weight – one well-greased rope for each pair, with a noose at each end – the one helping the other over the wall – a jerk down and a jerk up will send them to the home of their fathers. There let them hang till we come to Derby to cut them down.

THE KNIVES ARE OUT

Picketing began outside the factories, and this led to frequent fights. After one punch-up, two of the 'black sheep', nineteen-year-old Henry Ingram (one of the 'nine willing slaves' mentioned) and John Meakin, were charged with attempted murder. The victim survived the encounter, but had impressive knife wounds to display in court as evidence.

In his defence, Ingram complained that in the six months since he had been employed at the silk-hose factory he had hardly dared leave his lodging for fear of violence. He said they 'had scarcely ever left the factory without being insulted'.

One witness at the trial said that his doors and shutters were constantly bombarded, and that Union men had shouted murder threats and called him a 'bloody scab'. Another mentioned broken windows, threats of violence and beatings.

The mitigating circumstances and character references went well for Meakin, who was acquitted. Ingram, however, was found guilty and sentenced to death, in March 1834.

STARVED BACK TO WORK

The strike continued until April 1834, by which time Union funds had run out and families faced starvation. Many returned to work – but Frost and Peet refused to re-employ 600 of the strikers. For these men, tarnished by the Union tag, the workhouse beckoned...

There was better news for Henry Ingram. After appeal, his death sentence was transmuted to transportation for life, then reduced further to 'imprisonment in the Penitentiary for a limited period'.

1879

LADIES AND GENTLEMEN, FOR ONE NIGHT ONLY... KEITH'S CIRCUS!

THE STAR MUSIC Hall on Princes Street in Derby burned down in May 1873, following a play which included an on-stage fire as part of its drama. Making no attempt to learn from previous mistakes, the men who erected a new building on the site six years later ensured that it was shoddily designed, very draughty and built from prime tinder. Capacity crowds of 2,000 were possible, and given that the building was intended for performances from the highly popular Keith's Circus, fresh from their triumphs in Manchester, a full house would not be uncommon.

Circuses have always been big crowd-pullers in Derby, and in 1879 Keith's faced stiff competition in the town from 'Lord' George Sanger's troop, who had been putting on their shows in a classic 'big top' marquee. But the permanence of Keith's new building would surely give the company a certain advantage.

The newly arrived circus performers gathered even as the finishing touches were being put to their new venue, and such was the rush to get things ready for the opening night that proprietor Keith, so he later claimed, did not perform any safety checks on the fixtures and fittings. The circus employees did not even have time to go to their various lodgings, dumping all their worldly possessions backstage and getting ready for the first show.

BRINGING THE HOUSE DOWN

Sadly, the first show was also the last. Like its predecessor, the circus building burnt to the ground, in the early hours of 25 March 1879, after an opening night that had been strictly metaphorical in its desire to set the town on fire. Lasting less than twenty-four hours, this is the shortest-lived permanent circus in the history of the world.

The non-eagle eyes of a patrolling policeman and on-site security guard, Ralph Phineas 'Bill' White, failed to spot the telltale smoke, and by 5 o'clock in the morning the fire had taken such a hold that the combined efforts of firemen and police could not save the building. Their chief aim was to ensure that not too much of the neighbouring property joined in the conflagration. One of these adjoining buildings was a timber yard, with 'planks placed nicely for ignition', as a reporter noted.

The cries of the roasting animals within were briefly drowned by the collapsing of the corrugated iron roof. The firemen had been waiting for this moment, and once the roof was down they surged inside to

RECIPE FOR FIRE: TAKE ONE DRY WOODEN BUILDING, SEVERAL DODGY GAS FITTINGS, 100S OF SMOKING EMPLOYEES...

Derby's Music Hall and Circus were not the only victims of bad nineteenth-century fire regulations. Other disastrous blazes included:

* 1868 – The Cheese Factory
* 1886 – Derby Theatre
* 1888 – General outbreak in Wood's Lane
* 1890 – Holmes' Carriage Works
* 1890 – Kent's Flower Mills
* 1890 – Mitchell's Silk Mills
* 1896 – Sowter's Flour Mills
* 1897 – Sir T. Roe's Timber Yard

The latter was declared by the *Derby Mercury* 'the most serious conflagration which has occurred in Derby within the memory of its oldest inhabitant... nor do any of the other serious fires which have occurred in the town during this century compare with it in the amount of havoc wrought.' The fire, on Siddals' Road, destroyed many of the buildings surrounding the timber yard, and only demolition of strategic buildings prevented it from spreading further. Panicking householders threw furniture from their windows, adding to the chaos and the fuel. The 130 timber yard workers whose jobs had gone up in smoke had nothing but words of sympathy to console themselves with.

save any surviving animals, and to look for security guard Bill White. First out were the horses, who behaved calmly throughout, according to the newspaper report: 'The horses gave vent to no cries of terror, for trained as they have been, the dancing light would but appear as a special and extraordinary performance, through which they would pass with all decorum.'

Bill White was nowhere to be seen in the smoke, and hopes were raised that he had not actually been in the building during the fire. This made sense, for how else would he have failed to notice the blaze in the first place? Sadly, White *was* in the building, and had probably fallen asleep at his post. No witness had heard human cries, and it seems likely that White was killed by the fumes – although his remains were found near one of the internal doors, as if he had made a late bid to escape.

PHOENIX COAXED FROM ASHES

Less than an hour after the smoke had been spotted the fire was over, and only the building's doorway was left standing. White's charred remains were swept into a sheet and removed from the wreckage. The animal death toll included a monkey, a donkey, and twenty of the horses. Nothing inanimate was salvaged.

The cause of the fire was never determined. The presence of several dozen gas lamps and a thousand smokers in a basically wooden structure might give a clue, although the fire was judged to have started in the stables rather than the stage area.

Many Derbeians were sympathetic to the plight of uninsured proprietor Keith, and the Mayor launched a public subscription fund to salvage the business. Some of his less benevolent colleagues

'Lord' George Sanger's horses at auction in 1911. The mares in the photograph include Ida, a skewbald who specialised in counting cards and blowing out small flames. Sadly for Keith, however, she was not near his circus on the night in question...

argued against giving the circus people any extra money, arguing that such 'poor relief' as existed should be given to Derby townsfolk, not showmen and travelling folk who must accept their own risk and sort out their own problems. Several people resented the fact that circuses, fairs and the like attracted noise and criminality, and were happy to think that they had seen the last of Keith's Circus.

But these were in the minority. The public meeting agreed to set up the subscription, and Keith was suitably moved – no doubt overjoyed that he had faced his greatest calamity in a town which looked upon circuses as the ultimate in good nights out. Many people expressed sympathy for the horse trainers, and during the inquest many circus performers wept in court as the burning of the horses was described.

THE BURIED, THE BEREAVED AND THE BROKE

Keith's employees, who had dumped all their belongings in the building prior to the show, were told to expect generous recompense. There were less generous eulogies for poor Bill White, who, unbaptised, was buried in unconsecrated ground in the Nottingham Road cemetery, although the presence of his tragic fiancée at the funeral gave the newspapers something to latch on to. The minister from Derwent Street Chapel agreed to perform the service, and the undertaker provided his skills and hardware free of charge. The minister's sermon spoke out against men who saw this calamity as a judgement from God against pleasures of the low-brow kind: a gentle swipe against those who had opposed the subscription fund.

Keith gladly received the subscription money, raised at a time of great economic hardship in the town, and re-established his circus on The Holmes. A few months later, he was declared bankrupt and the show closed for the last time in July 1879. Sanger's, the smug lot in the big marquee, got their circus monopoly back. And is that a Sanger employee we see entering the Princes Street stables with a smouldering taper and quickly running out again? Only a conspiracy theorist would dream of suggesting such a thing.

THE BABY KILLER: DERBY'S FIRST AIR RAID

THE ENGINEERING TECH-NOLOGY of the First World War was not able to produce the kind of air raids that would flatten bits of Derby and much of Britain in the Second World War, but there was still an airborne assassin to be reckoned with: the Zeppelin, the first war machine to target innocents, and nick-named 'the Baby Killer'. These metal-framed monsters, along with the wooden-framed Schütte-Lanz airships, were never manufactured in bulk, just 140 taking to the air during the war. And in January 1916, nine of them were sent west from Germany with the intention of bombing key targets, chiefly in Liverpool.

Liverpool, however, was a long way away. The commander of the Zeppelin fleet, Alois Boeker, led the volatile airship fleet with a certain amount of trepidation inland from the Norfolk coast. A fully fuelled Zeppelin could manage 2,600 miles, and the journey to Liverpool, their furthest target, was only 500; but progress was ponderous. Top speeds of 60mph made this a slow-motion air raid, in spite of the chosen day, 31 January, having fairly favourable weather conditions of clear skies and just a light wind (anything stronger proving disastrous for these bulky vessels).

Each Zeppelin had twenty men on board, and each metal-skeletoned craft was kept airborne by several gasbags of hydrogen, each bag stitched from cows' intestines (known as 'goldbeater's skin' due to its development as a medium for beating gold into thin sheets). As any student of twentieth-century history, or any fan of Led Zeppelin album covers, knows, hydrogen is a highly volatile gas and will burst into flame at the least provocation.

Count Zeppelin, inventor of 'the Baby Killer', with the Kaiser.

AVIATOR ROYCE MISSES HIS FLIGHT

The founders of Rolls-Royce were the rich Charles Stuart Rolls, an aristocratic car dealer, and self-made engineer Frederick Henry Royce. It was an obvious marriage, with Rolls agreeing to sell the cars manufactured by Royce.

The first Rolls-Royce out of the factory was the Silver Ghost 1906, an instant iconic status symbol.

Royce had been hooked on flying since meeting the three Short brothers of Derby, who made balloons for, amongst others, the Government of India. He also befriended aeroplane pioneers the Wright Brothers, and his first flight was with Wilbur Wright.

Royce died on 12 July 1910 at a flying and landing competition at Hengistbury Airfield near Bournemouth. His aircraft, a Wright Flyer, suffered a break in the tail-end, and plummeted vertically to the ground. Royce was thrown clear on impact, but had received fatal head injuries. It is a sad irony that this engine pioneer did not survive into the era of Rolls-Royce as a lynchpin of the air force.

By 1914, Rolls-Royce had churned out hundreds of car engines. The War Office then asked the company to turn its attention to aircraft. By the end of the First World War, the company had fitted out dozens of aircraft, giving the country a fighting chance of keeping up with the Germans in the ongoing air race.

I HAVEN'T THE FOGGIEST...

Being something of a sitting duck for incendiary ammunition made any Zeppelin commander understandably nervous, which may go some way to explaining how Boeker failed to reach his intended destination. Perhaps the crews simply had bad maps and believed that they had indeed reached their target.

It also appears that the weather intervened, the Zeppelins encountering fog on the English coast to muddy their night vision even further. Radio contact was patchy, and the instruments – and men – inside the craft were prone to freezing. Zeppelins were hard to steer at the best of times, and some of the fleet encountered mechanical problems – probably due to ice. Whatever the reasons, they turned back somewhere east of Stoke on Trent and became scattered across the Midlands, shedding bombs here and there in a seemingly random fashion. Good news for Liverpool; less good for Derby. Perhaps Boeker's men knew that the Rolls-Royce engine factory was down there somewhere; or perhaps they had no idea they were over Derby. Either way, it looked like an obvious target.

At 11.45 p.m., a couple of Zeppelins released bombs at Swadlincote, ten miles south of Derby. A lone airship, wondering what to do with its remaining twenty-five weapons of mass destruction, hoved into view over Derby in the early hours of 1 February.

HIT AND MISS

The attack must have come as a great shock to the town. An early warning of the raid on the previous evening had led to successful black-out measures: the Zeppelins had passed within sight of the city on their way to Liverpool without dropping any bombs. This time, however, a few lights must have been switched back on. The Rolls-Royce factory, south of the town centre, was the first target. A direct hit would have had drastic consequences, as the company went on to produce 60 per cent of British-made aircraft engines in the war.

But the bomb missed, destroying a nearby street instead. Other weapons were discharged successfully at the Metalite Lampworks, the Carriage and Wagon Works and Fletcher's Lace Mill. One bomb landed without detonating in the garden of Litchurch Villa on the corner of Bateman Street. Most damage was done at the Midland Railway's locomotive works and the gas works at Etches Park.

Derby escaped with just five fatalities – three men killed at the locomotive works, with a fourth dying of injuries received, and a poor woman who allegedly died of a heart attack during the raid. The Zeppelin crew all returned home intact; and the Derby-bomber, an L14 type, actually survived the war. It was sabotaged by the Germans after their surrender, to prevent the technology falling into the victors' hands. Its passenger-bearing 'gondola' section was preserved in the museum at Berlin... only to be bombed to oblivion by the Allies in the next war.

Meanwhile, Boeker and his crew attended their debriefing after the raid, reporting that Liverpool had been successfully bombed. It was certainly better than the haphazard and messy truth. But did the commander actually believe that Derby was Liverpool? We will never know.

Hangar of death! A German airship under construction: part of the Kaiser's deadly fleet.

THE PRIME MINISTER MUST DIE! ALICE, THE DERBY ASSASSIN

THE STRUGGLE FOR social and moral reform in the nineteenth century, including the Acts that abolished slavery, prevented undue cruelty to children and animals, and delivered votes for working men, had been a protracted battle rooted in the radical thinkers of the previous century. But, by the turn of the twentieth century, the inexorable forces of progress had still not delivered suffrage for the biggest minority of all – women. For the men in power, the whole concept of women demanding rather than obeying was ludicrous and without social, historical, religious or scientific foundation. As uphill struggles go, this one was vertiginous.

But the battle was fought regardless, and none was more vigorous in the women's rights movement than Alice Wheeldon of Derby. She was a member of the Independent Labour Party, a force to be reckoned with in the Women's Social and Political Union (WSPU), and an outspoken pacifist who took every opportunity to denounce the warmongers precipitating conflict in Europe.

But war did indeed come, and one of its more overlooked consequences was that it brought an end to the campaign for women's suffrage. The movement had been pressing home its message both in print – *The Suffragette* newsletter – and on the

The struggle for rights for women was a desperate one. This image captures one of the most famous moments in the struggle: Emily Davison hurling herself underneath George V's horse, Anmer. She died of her injuries four days later.

streets via demonstrations, the chaining of oneself to fences, and through the accompanying leaked horror stories of arrested demonstrators being force-fed to foil their hunger strikes.

FAMILY CHEMISTRY

Alice Wheeldon's son William was a conscientious objector, not surprisingly, and the family received all the physical and verbal abuse associated with what was then a very controversial, lonely stance. His sisters Harriet and Winifred pitched in to the anti-war, pro-Left battle too, along with Winifred's husband Alfred Mason, every bit as determined as their (ironically warlike) matriarch.

Mason was a chemist, working in Southampton, and was named as co-chief conspirator with Alice Wheeldon in a thoroughly unlikely plot to poison Prime Minister David Lloyd George in 1917.

Alice would certainly have had no love for the PM and his Liberal Party – his foreign policy decisions having brought her campaigning efforts to an end, at least for the foreseeable future. Nobody wanted to hear women shouting about rights when the island itself was in danger of being conquered by foreign aggressors. But the accusations and evidence against Wheeldon have a strong cloak-and-dagger element, based as they are on the testimony of Government spies, who had doubtless been ordered to arrest these troublemakers, no matter what.

To the casual onlooker, Alice's family life was not that of the militant would-be assassin. Living as what we would now term a single mother, her husband having disappeared from the scene, she ran a second-hand clothes shop on Pear Tree Road, and her daughter Harriet taught Scripture in a school at Ilkeston. However, the radicalism was not far below the surface: Alice's shop served as a refuge

Lloyd George – Derby woman Alice Wheeldon was accused of trying to poison him.

for conscientious objectors; and Harriet's fiancé, Arthur MacManus, with active links to the Socialist Labour Party and the anarcho-syndicalist Industrial Workers of the World, helped smuggle them as refugees to Ireland and the USA.

DEADLY GAME OF DARTS

In January 1917, a package arrived at Alice Wheeldon's house. Inside were four vials of curare, a poison similar to strychnine, fresh from the chemist lab of her son-in-law Alfred Mason. Wheeldon always maintained that the poison was intended for guard dogs at the British concentration camps where conscientious objectors were held, to aid the prisoners' escape; but, unfortunately, her safe house for 'conshies' had been infiltrated by two Intelligence Services spies: Francis Vivian

DO YOU SWEAR...?

Middle-class Britain's distaste for communists, pacifists and moles, in Derby and the rest of the world, was overshadowed in the *Derby Mercury's* report of the Wheeldon case by an even more worrying presence in the courtroom: bad language.

It was a lamentable case, lamentable to see a whole family in the dock; it was sad to see women, apparently of education, using language which would be foul in the mouths of the lowest women. Two of the accused were teachers of the young; their habitual use of bad language made one hesitate in thinking whether education was the blessing we had all hoped.

Ironically, Harriet had refused to swear – in the legal sense, that is. She declared herself an atheist, turning the Bible, and its oath to God, away. This was not looked upon kindly by the jury – although, in being honest and 'coming out' as an atheist, her intention had been to demonstrate her commitment to telling nothing but the truth.

Mrs Pankhurst on the podium. She appeared at Alice Wheeldon's trial, but to no avail.

(also known as William Rickard) and Herbert Booth, who did not believe a word of it. It is upon their testimony that most of the ensuing court-case charges were based.

Alice, said her accusers, had intended using the curare to kill Prime Minister Lloyd George. This was to be done by the rather ingenious method of poisoning some airgun pellets and peppering the PM while he played golf in Surrey. Their suspicions had been aroused by some inflammatory words used by the Wheeldons in their covert communications: 'We will hang Lloyd George from a sour apple tree.' These communications were written in code, but the relevant letters had been intercepted and the code cracked by Vivian and Booth's men.

The pilfered poison was used as the pretext for arrest, and Alice Wheeldon and her two daughters were charged with conspiring to assassinate Lloyd George and Labour leader and War Cabinet minister Arthur Henderson, with 'poison darts'. It was a measure of the vilification that Wheeldon's anti-war stance received that she could find no British lawyer to defend her. A Persian, Dr Saiyid Haidan Riza, was the only one who offered his services.

NO GHOST OF A CHANCE

According to Harriet Wheeldon, it was the two Government spies who had suggested using the poison on Lloyd George. She had told them this was an absurd idea – not only because curare was not strong enough to kill anything bigger than a dog, but 'assassination was ridiculous, because if you killed one you would have to kill another and so it would go on'. The denial was backed up by prominent Suffragette Emmeline Pankhurst, who said in court that the WSPU believed 'there is no life more valuable to the nation than that of Mr Lloyd George. We would endanger our own lives rather than his should suffer.'

But the jury had no hesitation – Alice Wheeldon was found guilty, and could have been hanged for treason. She was given ten years in prison instead: perhaps the judge recognised the unmistakable whiff of a stitch-up. Winifred got five years, and chemist Alfred got seven, but Harriet was acquitted. That didn't stop her losing her job as a result of it all, though.

So, the dubious pellets were never fired, and key source of evidence, Vivian, died ten years later in a lunatic asylum: quite appropriate given that you needed to be mad to believe his story in the first place. But it was too late to save Wheeldon by then. Although she had been released on licence – largely to stop her grabbing headlines via a threatened hunger strike – in December 1918 (Winnie and Alf following her a month later), she had by then lost her shop and livelihood. She died on 21 February 1919 during the terrible flu epidemic, at London Road in Derby.

Her funeral was a sparse affair: a small gathering, no religious content, and a pro-Soviet political speech. The Suffragettes had to continue without her; however, her ghost is said to walk still, in the tunnels under the Guildhall where she was held before her trial.

THE SOVIET DERBEIANS: DEFECTION AND DEATH

Alice Wheeldon's son William emigrated to Russia after the war, where he became translator for the Executive Committee of the Communist International. Whether or not he wished to be buried on Soviet soil is unknown, but that was his fate.

With the formation of the USSR in 1922, Russian state security passed to a centralised body, the All-Union State Political Adminstration, or OGPU, forerunner of the infamous KGB. Whatever you wish to call it, it arrested Willie Wheeldon in 1937 on the orders of Josef Stalin. He had been a staunch supporter of Stalin's rival, Leon Trotsky.

Winifred and Alfred Mason appear to have been arrested at the same time. Alfred was by this time a Soviet citizen. Their fates are unknown.

Willie, however, was executed by firing squad.

ATTACK OF THE DECOY STARFISH

BEING TARGETED BY the Luftwaffe was bad news; but, as a town with a major war hardware manufacturer, Derby faced the prospect of sustained bombing with the kind of destruction not seen in these parts since Queen Ethelfleda burned the town to the ground more than a thousand years earlier. Its chief hope of survival lay in one of the Second World War's best kept secrets: Operation Starfish.

Intercepting German radio transmissions, jamming their radar and sending misleading rumours across the waves and airwaves were methods of deception that have been well documented since the Second World War ended. But Operation Starfish has been a bit more coy – even though it doubtless saved hundreds of lives.

Starfish was a very pragmatic operation – accepting the reality of Blitzkrieg but seeking to minimise the damage in the aftermath of the devastation unleashed in Coventry, which had been flattened. A German bomber searching for his target would be drawn towards a town that had already sustained hits – no amount of black-outs and other precautions could mask burning buildings. The goal of Operation Starfish, masterminded by the National Decoy Authority in July 1940, was to create a burning mock-town for those bombers to empty their hardware over.

USING ARSON TO PREVENT FIRE

Derby was one of the prime targets for an airborne attack due to the presence of the Rolls-Royce factory and its capacity for churning out aircraft engines. Zeppelins had attempted something similar in the First World War. The Starfish (whose title had evolved from the codename for the original concept, 'Special Fire') was established in the Belvoir Valley, as close to the middle of nowhere as you could get between Derby and Nottingham. A few mock buildings and several heaps of hastily harvested flammable material were laid out with the kind of super efficient slapdash that not even the best cowboy builder in the land could hope to emulate. As the Luftwaffe droned in, the site was torched – and, from high in the air, according to the theory, it would look like Derby, already merrily blazing.

The Belvoir Starfish had a twofold purpose: to impersonate Derby for the confounding of the enemy planes who were heading to the town, and to make the bulk of the invasion, which was destined for Nottingham, get its bearings wrong. And it worked well. Taking the Starfish Derby as a guide, the planes emptied their deadly cargo where Nottingham should have been, but wasn't. If you see what I mean.

COLLATERAL DAMAGE

Maurice Cooper-Key was killed as a result of his Hawker Hurricane suffering engine failure. During his emergency descent he altered course to avoid ploughing into children on the playing field at Balfour Road. He headed instead for open ground at the Barracks beyond Normanton and Peartree Station, but crashed into the railway embankment.

The black-outs imposed during the Second World War ensured that no light was visible to bombers looking for targets. But they also ensured that no light could be seen at ground level either. Kerbs and other exterior danger spots in Derby were subtly painted with white, enough to be seen by travellers in the dark, but not bright enough to give anything away from above. However, in spite of this precaution, accidents were commonplace. Many people were killed on the road, with blacked-out vehicles ploughing into blacked-out obstacles, including pedestrians. The year 1941 was the worst for this, both in Derby and in the country as a whole: over 9,000 people died in this way. In 1942 the Government introduced the 'look right, look left, look right again' kerb drill, as a direct response to the upsurge in road deaths.

An infamous enemy of Derby: Hitler, whose bombs were foiled by one of the strangest, and cleverest, schemes of the Second World War.

The Arboretum, Derby. This scene would be altered forever by the bombing raid of 1941.

Other cities benefited from Operation Starfish, including Sheffield, Bristol, Portsmouth and Birmingham. Derby's stand-in was one of the prototypes, and by the time the plan had been perfected, a blazing Starfish town had varied fire effects to make it more realistic from above. Different materials were used, such as wood, coal, creosote, paraffin and oil. Violent flashes of light replicating explosions were created by dousing oil boilers with water. It was quite some firework display, and the whole thing was ignited electrically by men in a nearby bunker. About 500 metres was deemed the safest distance – although not safe from the deadly deluge issuing from the fooled bombers above, of course.

In all, it is estimated that 730 decoys, including Starfish, had been bombed by 1944. Sadly, that did not stop the real Derby from receiving a battering. The town's first air-raid siren sounded just two days after the declaration of war – a false alarm, but the shape of things to come.

FACTORY IN DISGUISE

There were ten air raids on Derby in the Second World War. On 15 January 1941, 1,650 houses were damaged in a shower of fifty high explosives, and the Arboretum and railway station suffered too. Twenty died in the attack, and many more were injured.

Rolls-Royce was the Luftwaffe's main target. The Derby factory had developed the Merlin engine that powered Britain's air fleet of Spitfires and Hurricanes – an engine which was instrumental in winning the Battle of Britain. The Lancaster Bomber's four engines were also Merlins. If the Germans could take out the factory that produced these war machines, it would literally ground the British air force.

SOME OF THE LESS OBVIOUS CASUALTIES OF THE WAR

⨯⨯⨯

*   Barrage balloons, whose trailing wires were intended to deter low-flying bombers, flew over Derby throughout the war. One of them broke loose and got its hawser entangled on the lofty tower of All Saints' church (the city cathedral), tearing off one of the stone pinnacles.
*   Nearly all Derby's cast-iron fences and railings, those unifying features of pre-war towns, were taken away following one of the more dubious injunctions of the war effort. Streets and grand houses that had been regimentally railed like a huge Victorian zoo were afterwards free to replace these fixtures with whatever wood, wire, shrub or junk they saw fit. Surviving low walls with sawn-off iron stumps are a sad reminder of this overlooked form of secular desecration.
*   9,700 very unhappy children were evacuated from the town, mainly to outlying parts of remote Derbyshire.
*   On 29 May 1940, 350 Derby residents who were deemed undesirable due to their countries of origin were arrested without charge and sent for 'benevolent imprisonment' on the Isle of Man. This was in accordance with Defence Regulation 18b, which rounded up anyone under the vague tag 'of hostile origin or associations'. To add insult to injury, one of their fellow inmates in the prison camp was Sir Oswald Mosley, leader of the British Union of Fascists, and his wife, Diana. The Mosleys had strong links in Derby, and Diana's sister Deborah Mitford had married the man who was to become the 11th Duke of Devonshire. She was largely responsible for the renaissance of the Duke's Chatsworth House.

⨯⨯⨯

Rolls-Royce was ingenious in its self-defence, camouflaging the plant to resemble a village, with rows of houses, a chapel, a church tower, and water towers planted with trees. Had there not been a war behind these efforts, it would have been called an art installation, as it was designed by local painter Ernest Townsend – not exactly a household name, but probably Derby's most famous painter after eighteenth-century Joseph Wright. Only once was Rolls-Royce successfully hit, during a swift raid on 27 March 1942 by a Dornier 217 bomber. Twenty-two Derbeians lost their lives on that night.

SHERWOOD'S NON-MERRY MEN

Operation Starfish was assisted by successful attempts to jam the Luftwaffe's radar signal, and with hindsight it can be said that Derby got off relatively lightly. A total of seventy-four residents were killed, and about 350 injured, during air raids. But things did not go so well for local regiment the Sherwood Foresters. Many of them were trapped at, and evacuated from, Dunkirk in June 1940, and many more were taken prisoner in Singapore in January 1942, several dying horribly in the Japanese concentration camps.

For this reason, the Derby celebrations on VE Day, 8 May 1945, were very low key. Derbeians only celebrated with gusto on 15 August when two fateful, horrific bombs brought the conflict to a close on VJ Day.

BIBLIOGRAPHY

Primary sources

Derby Mercury, and other regional newspapers

The Times archive

The John Johnson Collection of Printed Ephemera

The Derbyshire Archaeological Journal, 1879–1994

Nottinghamshire and Derbyshire Notes and Queries, 1892–8

Defoe, Daniel, *A Tour thro' the Whole Island of Great Britain*, vol. ii, London, 1724; reprinted by J.M. Dent & Sons, London, 1928

Foxe, John, *The Book of Martyrs* (*Foxe's Book of Martyrs*), London, 1563

Garmonsway, G.N. (ed.), *The Anglo-Saxon Chronicle*, J.M Dent, London, 1972

Howell, T.B. (ed.), *A Complete Collection of State Trials and Proceedings for High Treason and Other Crimes and Misdemeanors, from the Earliest Period to the Year 1783*, London, 1816

Secondary sources

Britain Before the Norman Conquest, Ordnance Survey, Southampton, 1973

Craven, Maxwell, *An Illustrated History of Derby*, Breedon Books, Derby, 2007

Eddleston, John J., *The Encyclopaedia of Executions*, John Blake Publishing Ltd, London, 2004

Evans, Eric J., *The Great Reform Act of 1832*, second edition, Routledge, London, 1994

Noble, Thomas (Glover, Stephen, ed.), *The History, Gazetteer, and Directory of the County of Derby, in 2 parts*, Derby, 1829

Hutton, William, *The History of Derby, from the Remote Ages of Antiquity to the Year 1791*, London, 1791

Kirk, Peter, Felix, Peter and Bartnik, Gunter, *The Bombing of Rolls-Royce at Derby*, Rolls-Royce Heritage Trust, Derby, 2002

Simpson, Robert, *A Collection of Fragments Illustrative of the History and Antiquities of Derby*, 3 volumes, Derby, 1826

Sullivan, Paul, *The Peak District Year: A Derbyshire Almanac*, Churnet Valley, Leek, 2004

White, Francis, *History, Gazetteer and Directory of Derbyshire*, Sheffield, 1859

Websites

www.britannia.com

www.bygonederbyshire.co.uk

www.derbygaol.com

www.derbyshire-peakdistrict.co.uk

www.ghosts4u.com

The Oxford Dictionary of National Biography, www.oxfordndb.com

www.spartacus.schoolnet.co.uk

www.spondononline.co.uk

Wikipedia, en.wikipedia.org